# DAG HEWARD-MILLS

# LOYALTY & DISLOYALTY

Dealing With Unspoken Divisions Within the Church

LOYALTY & DISLOYALTY SERIES

Carpenter's Son Publishing

Published by Carpenter's Son Publishing, Franklin, Tennessee

Published in association with Larry Carpenter of Christian Book Services, LLC
www.christianbookservices.com

Edited by Paul Lewis

Cover and Interior Layout Design by Suzanne Lawing

Printed in the United States of America

978-0-9883962-2-7

# Dedication

To ***Rev. E. A. T. Sackey***, my friend and associate in ministry
Thank you for many years of faithfulness and loyalty.

# Table of Contents

## CHAPTER 1

# Matters of Loyalty

A rooster's cry pierced the early morning air. In Palestine, 33 A.D., it was nothing unusual, even in the high priest's Jerusalem court-yard. But this rooster's crow must have thundered in Peter's ears like a lightning strike. It was a stinging rebuke to his cowardice and disloy-alty. Moments earlier, in the face of simple questions from a maid at the door and a courtyard servant, Peter had three times denied even knowing Jesus, much less admitting to being his disciple.

The stare from Jesus across the courtyard must have been unforgettable--penetrating Peter to the core. What massive disloyalty to "the Master" he had just displayed. What could he have been thinking? How could he have denied his Savior?

Peter was only human, we reason. In that same moment you or I might have been equally scared and wondering whether loyalty was worth the risk. Perhaps Peter had forgotten that earlier in his ministry, Christ plainly laid out for him and every follower the high, costly and absolute require-ments of discipleship.

*"If anyone comes to me and does not hate his father and mother, his wife and children, his brothers and sisters--yes even his own life--he cannot be my disciple."* LUKE 14:26

**To Christ and in his Kingdom, loyalty reigns**

Loyalty is the foundation of discipleship and oh so vital in a healthy Church--the body of Christ. This is why I bring you this teaching on "Loyalty and Disloyalty". The Lord has laid this very core and practical subject on my heart for several reasons. First of all, repeatedly in the Word of God, I see the relevance of this subject. The Scriptures are replete with detailed accounts of faithful and treacherous people. There is a lot to learn from these stories in the Bible.

My few years in the ministry have also brought me face-to-face with loyal and disloyal people. I have noticed the impact that they have on churches and ministries. *In these pages I will share the reasons why understanding the dynamics of loyalty and disloyalty is of such relevant and profound importance to pastors and leaders in the church like you and me.*

## SEVEN REASONS WHY LOYALTY IS IMPORTANT

### 1. Loyalty is the principal qualification for every minister.

An inexperienced person is likely to think that the more gifted you are, the more qualified you are for the ministry.

My experience has shown me that it is the faithful and loyal people in church who are most qualified to be leaders.

**Friendly and Flashy!**

An inexperienced person would think that a friendly brother would make a good pastor. He may also think that someone with excellent oratory skills would make the best preacher. Do not make that mistake. The Bible teaches us that a cardinal requirement for leadership is faithfulness.

*...it is required in stewards, that a man be found faithful.*
1 CORINTHIANS 4:2

I have many wonderful pastors who work with me. Many of them are not overly friendly, flashy or particularly gifted. But time has proven that they are the best gifts God has given to His church and me.

## 2. To fight the fifth column

Very early in my ministry I realized that the devil is an expert at destroying the church from within. If you are a good minister, called of God, and doing the right things, the devil will have very little opportunity to fight against you from the outside. As Jesus said,

> ...the prince of this world cometh, and hath nothing in me.
> JOHN 14:30

You will realize that Satan often does not have the occasion to launch deadly outside attacks against you. Jesus was saying that though the enemy was coming after him, he did not have any grounds upon which to destroy him. There are many anointed preachers in this same category. Satan has no basis upon which to overcome them. So he has to use someone else to attack from within. In the case of Jesus, he used the traitor (Judas).

I recall reading the story of an army general who surrounded a large city with the aim of conquering it. This city was heavily fortified with a high and imposing wall and gate. The general's army surrounded the city in readiness to attack.

A friend of the general came along and asked him, "Sir, how are you going to overcome the defenses of this city? No one in recent history has been able to conquer this great city."

The army general smiled and said, "It's my fifth column. I'm depending on them to do the trick."

The general's friend was very interested and asked, "What is this fifth column? I thought you only had four columns."

The army general replied, "I do have a fifth column."

"Oh, I see. Is it a special commando unit, or are they airborne paratroopers?" the man asked.

### I Will Fight from Within

The general laughed, "No, it's none of these. My fifth column consists of my spies, agents, friends and supporters who are already within the city. You just wait. They will open those big gates from within, and my armies will rush in."

From within is the only way the enemy can destroy a successful and powerful ministry that is doing all the right things. It has to come from within. In every ministry a fifth column is comprised of disloyal, double-faced, double-tongued and discontented people. If allowed to wreak havoc as they so very well can, these people will destroy the church.

## I Had a Disloyal Associate

Years ago, when I started out in the ministry, I experienced the effects of having a disloyal associate. This person, although officially standing and working at my side, did not believe in me and was murmuring against me all the time.

His home was the meeting place for all the discontented people in the church. Every time they gathered, they would discuss and criticize me. They would talk about the way I preached. At other times, it would be the way I sipped water in the middle of my sermons. Some felt I was not friendly enough, etc. But the Lord revealed to me what was going on. So I prayed about it and asked the Lord what to do.

God told me, "Get rid of that guy."

I said, "Lord, do you mean he must leave the church?"

And the Lord said, "I mean exactly that! Dismiss him. Otherwise you will never have peace and your church will never grow."

I called for a meeting of the elders of the church. At the meeting I said, "I realize that Brother X is standing with them and not supporting me. He is constantly full of bitter criticisms."

I said to Brother X, "I know that you do not truly believe in my leadership anymore. I trained you. I brought you up. Yet today you are too big to remain under my authority."

I asked, "What do you think we should do?"

Then the brother said, "Let's work things out."

But the Scripture that the Lord had shown me quickly came to mind.

*Cast out the scorner, and contention shall go out; yea, strife and reproach shall cease.* PROVERBS 22:10

I spoke up, pointed to my assistant and said, "You know as well as I do that remaining here will not work out well--you don't believe in me anymore."

I went on, "Beginning today, I am relieving you of all your duties in this church."

He sputtered, "What!?" Then he said, "I will continue coming to church even though I may not have certain responsibilities."

## You Must Leave This Church Now!

But I said to him, "No! You must leave! You are not truly a part of us. Your continued presence in the church will only be destructive."

I tell you, it was no easy thing to dismiss a friend and associate of many years. But it had to be done. The Bible tells us that when Abraham was in conflict with Lot he directed Lot to go somewhere else! Abraham said, "If we are apart there will be peace and the work of God can go on."

A disloyal person breeds strife, hatred and murmuring. These disloyal sentiments are like smoke that fills an entire house. The only way to get rid of the smoke is to get rid of its source.

If you want to have a strong, prosperous and growing church, you must minister in love and with oneness. If real oneness is not a reality, stop pretending. You see, with compassion and sensitivity, I encourage people to walk out of my church if their hearts are not with me and the others in leadership.

*He that is not with me is against me...* MATTHEW 12:30

If I have to, I will beg you to leave. I am serious about this. I will even give you money for your transportation and snacks as you leave us! It is so that those of us who love one another and are confident about each other can remain united and continue working.

## Get Rid of Pretenders

I don't know how to pretend. I simply don't know how to do it. But there are many pretenders in the church. They pretend to love you and support you, but in their hearts they despise you.

### 3. For the love of God to fill the church

Christian ministry is supposed to be marked by the power of love, unity and teamwork.

> *By this shall all men know that ye are my disciples, if ye have love one to another.* JOHN 13:35

To minister effectively as leaders, we must exhibit the love that Jesus spoke about. People are attracted to love. When they see leaders who flow together in genuine love, they want to join in. You must never forget that your church members are not blind. Neither are they deaf. They can see and sense the disunity and discord when it is there.

### Sheep Drink from Still Waters

One thing that every pastor must know about sheep is that they only drink from still waters. If the water is murky and rough, the sheep will stay away. You see, they are not sure there is not an alligator or snake in the water!

> *...he leadeth me beside the still waters.* PSALM 23:2

Whenever there is treachery and distrust, your church members become wary and stay away.

### 4. To have a successful ministry and ministerial team

Of course, one man can only do so much. One pastor can only be at one place at a time. He can only minister until his strength (which is limited) is exhausted.

Because of this, anyone who wants to extend his ministry and bear much fruit must work with many other people. These people make up the team that I'm talking about. **But it would be better to work alone than with a team of disloyal, disgruntled, disunited and disaffected people.** In fact, there cannot be an effective team with such people. I have only been able to accomplish what I have only because of the team with whom I work.

### 5. To have a mega church

As I write this, there are Lighthouse churches all over the world – Ghana, South Africa, New York and Switzerland to mention just a few. These churches are part of a network that is loyal to the Lighthouse headquarters in Ghana, Africa. Often people will ask me, "How do you sustain churches in all these different locations? What controls do you have?"

I explain, "Yes, there are standards and expectations clearly spelled out, but at its core, maintaining the system of many Lighthouse churches relies on loyalty. The churches are pastored by ministers who are loyal to the Lord, to me and to the Lighthouse vision.

**Without loyalty, every local church, ministry within the church, or a network or denomination of churches will constantly experience disintegration.** At any level they will inevitably divide into splinter groups and or smaller sub-churches, as the case may be.

### Their Church Disintegrated

I remember the saga of a branch church that disintegrated because of disunity. Some long-standing seeds of disloyalty manifested themselves shortly after a fundraising event in the local church. As a result of this disagreement, the pastor decided to resign and start his own church. He was actually so angry that he returned all the monies he had raised. The church members of course were very surprised that the money they had given to the church was being returned.

This pastor spread many bad stories about his denomination and its senior ministers. Naturally, this church virtually disintegrated following the disloyal and disastrous actions of this pastor.

Dear friend, I could recount story after story of why churches (especially branch churches in big cities) and sub-ministries within local churches often divide and break off. **Without principled and loyal pastors and church workers, the ministry of our Lord's Church will always become tarnished and limited.**

## 6. To have a long-lasting ministry

In the larger picture, a person generally has but a few years of extremely practical and effective ministry. Jesus ministered for only three-and-a-half years, but he extended his ministry and his influence through his effective and loyal team. Notice that Jesus' ministry has reached into the whole world and spanned almost 2,000 years.

If I were to die today, the Lighthouse Chapel will live on! It does not depend on me. I have not built a church around my personality. The church will continue. Not one of us is indispensable. God can do without us. But this is why we need to build a team of loyal successors.

## 7. In order to reap our full reward

Those who benefit from the blessings of success are the faithful and loyal ones in Christ's Church. One day, we all hope to hear those wonderful words, "Well done, good and faithful servant." In ministry, those who stick with you through stormy or difficult times are different from those who work and stay only when everything is going smoothly.

### Well Done!

Jesus himself told his 12 disciples that they would be treated differently from any other famous minister. They would have a special kingdom and their names would even be written on the foundations of the New Jerusalem.

> *And the wall of the city had twelve foundations, and in them*
> *the names of the twelve apostles...* REVELATION 21:14

Even great men of God we know today will not qualify for this special reward. Jesus explained the reason for this special reward: they had been loyal to him through the most difficult part of his ministry.

> *Ye are they which have continued with me in my temptations...*
> *I appoint unto you a kingdom...* LUKE 22:28, 29

Loyalty, you see, is most appreciated in the hard times. In the good times everybody is (or appears to be) loyal.

### A Few Have Stood

I cannot begin to express enough my gratitude to the pastors who have stood with me throughout my ministry. They have watched me rise and supported me, even in my mistakes. To me, they are different from all the others. I know you feel the same way about every loyal coworker who has served with you any level of ministry--large or small. Like Jesus said, they have a special reward!

# Matters of Loyalty

*(For reasons of privacy you may want to make notes on a photocopy of this page.)*

## Chapter One - My Action Plan:

1. List the one or two ideas about loyalty that most caught my attention:

2. What point(s) or ideas about loyalty need my further thought?

3. When and how has disloyalty impacted my ministry, church, organization?

4. For a few minutes or over lunch, with whom should I discuss this chapter's key points? When? (As preparation, share the chapter with that person(s).)

CHAPTER 2

# Slipping into Disloyalty

## BECOMING DISLOYAL IS A PROCESS

Disloyal thoughts and actions don't surface overnight. Becoming disloyal is a process! Most people are unaware they are becoming disloyal. Many leaders do not even recognize early disloyalty in their associates. Let me show you the stages a person moves through as he is or she gradually changes into a rebel.

### Learning to Detect Disloyalty

There are two reasons why you must know these eight steps or stages to disloyalty. First of all, they will help you identify and kill any tendencies toward disloyalty within yourself. **Secondly, they will help you to detect disloyalty in a person you work with,** whether in a ministry setting, or even in businesses, particularly in a smaller company.

The Lord has shown me eight important stages a person progresses through when he or she is becoming disloyal. The first stage is to develop what I call an independent spirit.

## STAGE ONE: THE INDEPENDENT SPIRIT

The independent stage is so subtle most people do not recognize it for what it actually is --disloyalty. When a person belonging to a group, ministry or company develops an attitude of unhealthy independence, he or she becomes more and more autonomous within the setup. The rules of the organization no longer control his or her behavior. While still an active part of the church, this person does what he or she wants to do in spite of contrary instructions.

For instance, the pastor may say, "We are all fasting on Friday." But this person with an independent spirit reasons, "I've already decided to fast on Wednesday. So that's what I'll do."

### Watch out for the Independent Ones

Pastors, watch out for deacons and church leaders, and keep an eye out for coworkers and volunteers who have independent spirits. You may schedule several meetings, but the person with an independent spirit will decide to attend only those he or she feels are important. This person obeys only certain instructions, requests or guidelines from you – the ones he decides are truly important.

If you are unfortunate enough to have choir members who have independent spirits you may experience something like this. You schedule vital prayer meetings, rehearsals and outreaches, but an independent chorister decides, "I think I'll just attend the rehearsal." This individual does only what he or she thinks is important to be done.

Now, there is nothing wrong with being independent. I believe in independence. *Correctly understood,* independence is a vital character strength, and we thank God for the capacity to think and act independently in the right way and spirit. **However, if you are a part of a denomination, group or company, you are not completely independent.** You want the ministry or organization to benefit from your presence and efforts, so you have chosen to submit and exchange some of your autonomy for the overall good of the mission of the church or organization.

When you begin to exhibit an undisciplined spirit of independence within an organization, you are becoming disloyal.

### I Had an Independent Spirit

Many years ago, I belonged to a group that had branches all over the country. I even founded a branch of this group. As time went on, I began to have difficulties and disagreements with those in leadership at the headquarters of this group.

At that time, I thought my superiors at the headquarters were out of step spiritually. You see, the branch group I was leading was growing. Many souls were being established every week.

The overall directors of the organization would call for meetings at the headquarters. They wanted every branch group to come into town for these meetings. But I never went to the meetings and didn't encourage any of the members of my branch to attend.

I always reasoned to myself, "Those meetings are not important. What I am doing on this branch campus is important. I am winning souls."

### I Was Wrong

But, I was wrong. I had an independent spirit and didn't even recognize it. The overseers found me to be a successful leader in my little branch, but they could not control me within the organization. At that time, I just attributed the conflict to lack of vision on the part of my overseers.

The point I'm making is this: **If you belong to an organization, you are not completely independent of that organization. Therefore, you cannot just do only what you think is right.** You must comply with directives coming from the leadership. If you feel you want to be more independent, then you should resign.

### Pastor Joab – The Independent Killer

Were there people in the Bible with an unhealthy spirit of independence? The answer is yes. Throughout the Second Book of Samuel, Joab is described as someone who did what he wanted to do. He was part of David's army. You might say he was part of David's ministry team. He was one of David's managers! He was the Prime Minister, or David's right-hand man. He was very powerful, yet he had an independent spirit. And this independent spirit manifested itself many times.

The first example of Joab's independence was in the murder of Abner.

Abner was commander-in-chief of another section of the armies of Israel. David, as the head of government, decided to make peace with Abner after years of conflict.

The King even called for celebrations of this peace agreement by feasting with Abner.

> *So Abner came to David... And David made... him a feast...*
> *and he went in peace.*  2 SAMUEL 3:20, 21

But when Joab heard that Abner had been entertained in the palace, he was furious. He chased him, caught up with him and requested to speak with him privately. It was a trick, and Joab killed him.

> *And...he [Joab] sent messengers after Abner, which brought him*
> *again... took him [Abner] aside... and smote him...*
> 2 SAMUEL 3:26, 27

When the King opted for peace, his right-hand man decided to do otherwise. Although he was supposed to submit to the wishes of the king, he went ahead with his own plan. People like this are dangerous. **Joab could have plunged an entire nation into war through his independent actions.**

There are people like that in church. The founder or Head pastor often shapes and carries the vision. He leads the way because that is the responsibility of the role he plays. All associate pastors and leaders in the church must support and flow with the leader's vision. An independent 'Pastor Joab' will only cause confusion and strife in the church. Leaders must take note of such people serving under them in the church or in their organization, because they are only a few stages away from open rebellion.

The second incident I want you to notice is in Joab's handling of Absalom's coup d'état.

### Rev. Joab Goes Independently Again

Absalom rebelled and actually ousted his father, David, from the throne. Absalom was now in power, and David was faced with the bizarre circumstance of having to fight against his own son.

In the midst of these extraordinary circumstances, David specifically instructed his army that they should not kill his son Absalom. He wanted to spare the life of his son.

> *And the king commanded Joab… Deal gently for my sake*
> *with… Absalom…* 2 SAMUEL 18:5

Thankfully, the battle turned in the favor of King David, and Absalom had to flee. A certain man reported that he had seen Absalom hanging from a tree by his hair. Joab immediately blurted out, "Why didn't you kill him? I would have rewarded you handsomely."

But the man said,

> *…Though I should receive a thousand shekels of silver in mine*
> *hand, yet would I not put forth mine hand against the king's*
> *son: for in our hearing the king charged thee… saying, Beware*
> *that none touch the young man Absalom.* 2 SAMUEL 18:12

This unnamed person was part of King David's command and was obviously loyal to him. But here comes a man with an independent spirit and look at what happened.

### Independent People Do What They Want to Do

> *…And he [Joab] took three darts… and thrust them through*
> *the heart of Absalom…* 2 SAMUEL 18:14

Independent people do what they want to do despite the instructions emanating from above.

### Ironically, Independent People Don't Leave

Notice that Joab never really left David's camp. Such people often decide not to leave. They stay around but *do only what they want to do!* This is the definition of the independent spirit, and it is a degree of disloyalty.

I always notice independent people within the congregation. Some of them are leadership material but because they are independent of me and of my vision, I cannot afford to work with them.

### He Was Spiritual, but Independent

I once asked an independent church member, in whom I saw leadership potential, to join our Bible school. His response was characteristic of an independent person. He said, "I have been in the church since it began many years ago. I have heard all of your messages."

He continued, "Pastor, what else am I going to learn in this Bible school?" That was the end of the matter. He didn't attend.

Another time, I asked him to become a fellowship (cell) leader within the church. He told me, "Pastor, I am already conducting a fellowship in my home."

I asked, "Who are the members of this fellowship? Are they members of our church? Do you consider this to be a church group?"

"Oh no!" he answered. "They are my personal converts."

This brother could not be a cell leader within the church because he was building his own private cell group. He had no intention of defecting from the church. He was within the church but independent of all that was going on around him.

### Branch Pastor Joab Threatens a Takeover

The next example of Joab's independence was when he fought against the royal city of Rabbah on behalf of King David. When victory was in sight he sent a warning message, "You better come and participate in the war. Otherwise I will get all the credit."

> *Now therefore gather the rest of the people together, and encamp against the city, and take it...* 2 SAMUEL 12:28

He wanted David to be there himself! What he was saying in so many words was, "I'm no fool to do all the hard work only for you to take the glory." As we say in Ghana, "Monkey dey work, baboon dey chop". (The monkey does all the hard work while the baboon gets the reward.)

### Pastor Threatens to Change the Church's Name

Joab went on to threaten that if the king did not get involved as he was suggesting, the city could be named after him instead of David.

*...lest I take the city, and it be called after my [Joab] name.*
2 SAMUEL 12:28

How could a leader send such a message: "Come quickly otherwise I will change the name of the church"? Such a pastor can take over a branch church and rename it. Such a person can convert a cell group into his personal church. This is unfortunately the reason some pastors don't believe in cells or branches. They fear that they will have Joabs as leaders.

The last example of Joab's independent spirit comes at the end of the king's life. David made it very clear that he wanted Solomon to be the next king.

### Independent Pastor Helps the Opposition

There was another son named Adonijah who wanted to be king instead of Solomon. To do this he needed the help of some perfidious characters. Once again Joab, who knew David's wishes, went contrary to them and helped Adonijah.

*Then Adonijah… exalted himself, saying, I will be king... And he [Adonijah] conferred with Joab … [who] helped him.*
1 KINGS 1:5, 7

## STAGE TWO: OFFENSE

The second stage of disloyalty is offense. Jesus said,

*And then shall many be offended, and shall betray one another, and shall hate one another.* MATTHEW 24:10

From this Scripture you can see that people begin to betray and hate one another when they are offended. The Bible says folks will betray you when they are offended. **I have always been wary of wounded people because I know that they can more easily turn against me. The spirit of offense opens the door to the spirit of treachery.**

### Is Anyone Hurt?

Dear pastor and leader, look around you and observe those who have been wounded by one event or another. If these people have not genuinely overcome their hurts, hear the voice of the Spirit today. They are potential separatists, and they can become a problem in your midst--even your enemies.

I believe that Absalom was grievously hurt by two important events. The first was his half-brother's rape of his sister. He probably decided on the very day it happened to kill this half-brother.

The second event was that his father, King David, did not take the appropriate action against Amnon for raping Tamar. The Bible says King David was very angry with Amnon. However, he was under obligation to do more than just being angry. If he had done his duty, he would have fulfilled the Law of Moses.

> *And if a man shall take his sister, his father's daughter... and see her nakedness... [he] shall be cut off...* LEVITICUS 20:17

The penalty for incest in those days was death. But David failed to meet it out. Please never forget this: Unresolved hurts and offenses can push people down the path to disloyalty.

## STAGE THREE: PASSIVITY

After being offended by something, people become passive.

When a person at the passive stage of the disloyalty does not involve himself in much, he sits and watches unconcerned and uninvolved. Leader, look out for people in the congregation or your organization who are indifferent and unconcerned. They are much more likely to abandon ship.

### Watch out for the Uninvolved Members

For instance, I consider regular members to be passive if they don't get involved in prayer meetings or smaller group activities. When a meeting is called for all businessmen, he is not likely to attend, even though he is a businessman. Such people may have been hurt in the recent past. They often think or say things like, "I don't want any more trouble in this church. Let me just keep to myself."

*Cursed be he that doeth the work of the Lord deceitfully, and*
*cursed be he that keepeth back his sword from blood.*
JEREMIAH 48:10

You can see from this Scripture that God expects you to get involved when you have something to contribute. This verse is actually telling us that it is a curse to be uninvolved when you have a relevant gift or experience, or something to add.

Passivity is dangerous because it moves you rapidly toward the stage of being critical. **In order to become critical, you must be uninvolved. You must have enough time to scrutinize and despise the church (or organization) and its leaders.** An uninvolved person more readily sees the faults of things and others around him?

As a Ghanaian saying observes, it is the bystander who sees that the worker is digging a crooked trench. All leaders must learn to look for signs of passivity among their workers. The uninterested coworker or leader is uninvolved for a reason.

### Why Was He So Quiet?

Remember the story? Absalom went through this stage of passivity. Amnon had raped and disgraced Absalom's sister, Tamar. Absalom was undoubtedly angry with his half-brother but said nothing for two whole years. That is passivity! Doing nothing and saying nothing! I do not overlook silent and detached people who have nothing to say or contribute.

*And Absalom spoke unto his brother Amnon neither good nor*
*bad...* 2 SAMUEL 13:22

But notice again that this indifferent person (Absalom) quickly degenerated into a murderer and equivocated when the opportunity presented itself.

*...Absalom had commanded his servants... when Amnon's*
*heart is merry with wine... then kill him...* 2 SAMUEL 13:28

**Are You Happy?**

When I talk about being "quiet," I am not talking about someone who has a naturally subdued personality. I am talking about someone who is normally outgoing but is intentionally subdued and detached.

One of the questions I regularly ask those around me is, "Are you happy?" I want people around me to be upbeat and enjoying themselves. I am concerned when someone is unusually calm and cool. Every good leader must ensure that those around him are secure and content. **If King David had noticed Absalom's nonchalant attitude, he might have been able to prevent his son from becoming a full-fledged anarchist.**

## STAGE FOUR: THE CRITICAL STAGE

A disloyal person is not passive forever; he progresses on the stage of being critical. This is evidenced by the noticing and magnifying of faults. In church, he finds faults with the preaching of the Word and with the order of service. He analyzes the building and notices all the deficiencies of the surroundings.

Miriam had become critical of Moses. She had followed his leadership all the way out of Egypt, but now she began to see his faults and humanness. She spoke about his marital problems.

*And Miriam and Aaron spake against Moses...* NUMBERS 12:1

I remember early in my ministry, a spirit of disloyalty entered the church. Many of the church members became very critical of me. With eagle eyes they watched for my faults. Poor me!

### I Was Frightened by My Church Members

I was a young pastor with no theological training. And here I was, being subjected to the critical scrutiny of these people.

"Is he really called?" they asked.

"Can a medical student be a pastor?"

I could virtually hear them saying, "We know you don't have much to say. Just summarize your message and let's close the service."

### I Dreaded Saturday Evenings

I would become so nervous on Saturdays that I would have diarrhea from Saturday night to Sunday morning. Once I asked my beloved (fiancé), "Is this the dread I will have to go through every Saturday night?"

I will never forget standing before the congregation, on one particular Sunday morning. I lifted my eyes from my Bible after praying, and saw the angry and hypercritical eyes of my assistant and a host of others. I knew within me that they would never find anything good in what I was about to preach. This critical atmosphere almost broke up my fledgling church.

Naturally, a hypercritical atmosphere does not help anyone to preach well. Some may ask why I teach so much on the subject of loyalty. This is because I have experienced the devastating impact disloyalty can have on the ministry, a church and any organization.

### Point of View or Viewpoint?

Someone once told me that your point of view depends on your viewpoint. The value of something varies depending on how you look at it. **If you look at something with critical eyes, you will only see the imperfections.** But, if you look at it with through eyes of love you will see something good with value for the future.

Absalom had begun to find faults with the king's style of leadership. He was so engrossed in the deficiencies of David's ministry that he could see no good anywhere. This only led to the next stage of disloyalty – deception.

*And Absalom said unto him, See, thy matters are good and right;*
*but there is no man deputed of the king to hear thee.*
2 SAMUEL 15:3

## STAGE FIVE: THE POLITICAL STAGE

When a person becomes political, he seeks to involve others in his ideas and philosophies. Politicians operate on the power of people's opinions. Many politicians don't tell the truth because they want to please people. What people think and want is what concerns them most.

A person who is becoming disloyal tries to involve other people in his treacherous ideas. **He wants to gather a following and make people believe that he has identified a real problem that must be addressed.** This is exactly what Absalom did.

Absalom was hurt (Offense stage), and then he said nothing for two years (Passive stage). He then became unduly analytical of David's policies (Critical stage). Now he began to involve other people in his disloyal thoughts.

> *And Absalom said unto him, See, thy matters are good and*
> *right; but there is no man deputed of the king to hear thee.*
> 2 SAMUEL 15:3

The Bible tells us that Absalom sat at the gate of the city. When anyone came to see the king, he would ask if they had any problem. He would then listen carefully and sympathize with them.

He explained to the people, "It is a pity that the king has no time for you today."

He lamented, "Unfortunately, he has not even bothered to delegate someone to attend to your problems."

### Let's Pray for our Pastor

Absalom went on, "Let's pray for our dear king. He's getting older and is probably finding it difficult to cope with the job." This is a mistake some associate pastors make. Because of their work schedule they may have more opportunity to interact with the people. The congregation begins to feel that the associate is more accessible and friendlier than the senior pastor (the king) is.

The associate becomes deceived into thinking that his more frequent interaction with the people makes him a better pastor than the senior pastor and therefore is to be chosen over or preferred over the senior. The associate intentionally makes certain allusions and insinuations, etc. about the senior pastor (the king) that undermine him – suggesting that he is incompetent and really just a figurehead.

The people of Israel were so impressed with the king's son for two reasons. First, he was so handsome and physically attractive. Second, he seemed to genuinely care for them. After impressing them for a while, Absalom won the hearts of the people.

> ...*So Absalom stole the hearts of the men of Israel.*
> 2 SAMUEL 15:6

When someone becomes political he wants to involve others in his train of thought. You see, the more people that you can involve in something controversial, the more confidence you gain.

**Disloyal people have an insidious way of discussing the shortcomings of their leaders.**

They ask questions like, "How did you like the service today? I thought it was a bit dry."

They even come up with Scriptures: "As a Bible-based church, don't you think we should see some miracles?"

"Do you think our pastor is as anointed now as he was last year?"

"Have you noticed that a lot of people are leaving the church?"

"I think that our pastor travels a bit too much. Don't you?"

These questions are used as bait for unsuspecting Christians. They drag innocent members into analysis of issues that are not their responsibility or concern.

> ...*neither do I exercise myself in great matters, or in things too*
> *high for me.* PSALM 131:1

Gradually they are able to spread their dissenting feelings to a group of gullible Christians.

### Many People Are Saying...

Next, they approach you with reports of discontent within the congregation. From experience, I have learned that a person in the political stage of disloyalty has three favorite phrases:

• A lot of people are saying "such-and-such."

• Everybody is saying "such-and-such."

• Many people are saying "such-and-such."

They say, "A lot of people are saying, 'You travel too much.' Everybody is saying that the church building project has taken too long to complete."

They explain, "I am speaking on behalf of many who are not happy in church."

### His Home Was the Centre of Discussion

Some years ago, I had an associate just like that! He seemed friendlier than I was and more accessible. People would take their problems to him. His home was the center for the discussion of the problems of the church. They discussed all of my shortcomings. The church members became more and more discontent with my style of doing things.

"He preaches too long, don't you think?"

"He sips water while he preaches."

"He walks up and down too much."

With time, he began to tell me, "A lot of people are saying... Many people are saying..."

### There Is Joy and Liberty When He Travels

I recall one day I was away at a retreat center for a time of fasting and prayer. I happened to see there the associate pastor of a large church in my city. After exchanging social pleasantries, I asked, "How is your senior pastor?"

"Oh, he's around," he said.

I went on, "How is the church doing?"

He replied, "We have some problems, but we are watching. You know what, *when he travels everybody is happy.*"

Confused, I asked, "When who travels?"

He smiled and said, "The senior pastor."

"Why is this so?" I queried.

He answered, "Because when he's away there is liberty and joy, and the Holy Spirit flows. The fact is that, *a lot of people are not blessed anymore when he preaches.*" He emphasized, "Oh, many people are not happy when he is here! There is joy and liberty when he is away!"

As I listened to him, I concluded that this man was well down the path of disloyalty. And I was not wrong! Less than a year later, he rebelled and broke away from his senior pastor, taking a portion of the church with him.

### Sack Him!

When a person arrives at this political stage of disloyalty, he becomes dangerous to the unity and stability of the church. And such an individual is a threat to the security of your leadership.

It is unsafe to maintain this "Absalomic" personality within your ranks. In my opinion, you have more than enough biblical grounds to get rid of him.

## STAGE SIX: DECEPTION

One thing I am sure about is that people who rebel are grossly deceived. If they were not deceived, they would not do some of the things they do -- most end up in destruction. And no one intentionally sets out to destroy his life.

Let's walk through some of the common deceptions that ministers and leaders encounter as along the road to disloyalty. And please realize that every minister is also tempted with these thoughts.

**Many rebellious people are deceived into thinking they are greater than their seniors.** Sometimes a son in the ministry can rise up to do greater things than his father. Jesus did not seem to be worried about the fact that some of his disciples would do more miracles. He actually predicted that his trainees would do greater things than he had done, and he was happy about it.

> *...the works that I do shall he do also; and greater works than these shall he do...* JOHN 14:12

History has shown this to be true. Today, evangelists minister to crowds much greater than Jesus ever did. Ministers have larger Bible schools than Jesus did (Jesus had only 12 students in his Bible school). Jesus never travelled more than 200 miles from the place where he was born. I have travelled thousands of miles from where I was born. Jesus never wrote a book, but you are reading one of my numerous books. Jesus never had an office for his ministry, but most churches do. Jesus never went to the university, but I did for seven years.

Jesus raised only two people from the dead, but some faith healers claim to have raised many people from the dead. At the end of his life, Jesus was ruthlessly murdered by his enemies and condemned amongst thieves. Most pastors receive an honorable exit from this world. But Jesus didn't have that!

While he was dying, the soldiers gambled for one of the few personal possessions he had on earth -- his coat. Most ministers these days own far more property on this earth than Jesus did.

These facts do not make any of us greater than Christ. Christ is still Christ the King. And you and I are still mortal non-entities. Without Him we are nothing. But do not be deceived by a recent honor or promotion in the ministry or organization. You are still you.

Jesus said,

> ... *The servant is not greater than his lord; neither he that is sent greater than he that sent him.* JOHN 13:16

It is unfortunate that too often when we make little gains in the ministry, we begin to think that we are greater than others or those who have gone before us.

### Don't Despise Your Teacher

Ministers come to despise their mentors or teachers just because they have acquired a little following and a new car or some other symbol of status. One of the oaths I had to take as a new doctor was to respect my teachers. You must remember that you have been helped by somebody to get to where you are. You must never forget that, in a certain sense, you have been set where you are by or through someone else.

God appointed Lucifer, but it seems he forgot that all-important fact.

> *Thou art the anointed cherub... and I have set thee so...*
> EZEKIEL 28:14

Lucifer forgot that his perfection, wisdom and beauty had come from God. He was created, not the Creator. You learn what you know from someone. Eighty percent of what we preach and teach is learned. Lucifer did not create himself.

> *…Thou… full of wisdom… perfect in beauty… wast created.*
> EZEKIEL 28:12, 13

Some people gain a little vision and go off the deep end. Some pastors see a few miracles in their churches, and from that time on, they respect no one. They lay hands on one or two people who fall under the power of the Spirit, and their hearts become corrupted by this success in the ministry. Many sing their praises. Young ladies approach them with admiring eyes.

### Deceived by His Recent Success

Listen as the Prophet Ezekiel describes the delusion and fall of Satan:

**Thou are the anointed cherub that covereth, and I have set thee so; thou wast upon the holy mountain of God; thou hast walked up and down in the midst of the stones of fire.**

**Thou wast perfect in thy ways from the day that thou wast created, til iniquity was found in thee.**

> *Thine heart was lifted up because of thy beauty…*
> EZEKIEL 28:14-15, 17

In my country of Ghana, many pastors become rebellious when they are sent outside their country to pastor churches in rich European and American cities. They walk up and down in the midst of the "stones of fire," and it goes to their heads.

It is quite a wild and impressive feat, so sometimes pastors exposed to and given access to the corridors of power in rich and exotic places become swollen headed.

Ezekiel refers to this in relation to Satan and suggests that it contributed to his deluded state, in that it was part of the privileges he had by virtue of his position, a position that God created and placed him there.

These days, maybe a pastor is asked to moderate the service, or lead praise and worship at a major event, and because of that they feel they have arrived.

Or a pastor has been transferred from a branch to the Headquarters or from Accra, Ghana to New York in America to pastor a church. Such a move is then erroneously interpreted by the pastor to be a major promotion and then he forgets he was 'made,' in the sense given the opportunity, and if it were not for that, he would not even be there in New York.

I remember one minister who had been in training for some years. He was sent to pastor a branch church for the first time in his ministry. After six months, he returned completely transformed into a rebel.

### He Said, "Give Me Six Months"

No one could control or counsel him. He had cutting rebukes for his seniors, pointing out to them that they were not always right.

This person had become deceived into believing he was as gifted as anyone else was. In the end, he resigned, bitterly denouncing and deriding his superiors in the ministry. Out of contempt, he called his former church a cult. He even went as far as calling his father-in-the-Lord (the one who led him to Christ) a fool for associating with the church he was leaving.

To emphasize the "I'm as good as you are" attitude, he started a church nearly adjacent to his home church. And he began to invite members from his previous denomination to join him.

That was not all. This refractory anarchist vowed to prove his ministerial gift to everyone within six months of his defection. However, years after this defiant separatist revolted, he has simply disappeared into obscurity.

This obstinate insurgent thought that within six months he could achieve things that take many years of experience to attain.

I believe avoiding deception was one of the reasons why Jesus instituted the Lord's Supper. It is to remind each of us at whatever level of ministry or leadership, that no matter what you achieve or attain, you are not Christ! We must remember our origins. We must remember how we became what we are today. Jesus said,

> ...*this do in remembrance of me.* LUKE 22:19

Many rebellious people are deceived by their giftedness and anointing. Absalom was very gifted but wanted to be the king. Many insurrectionists mistakenly think that they have acquired all the knowledge they will ever need.

### The Mother of All Deception

The mother of all deception is when the mutineer believes he can destroy his teacher and father. He thinks he has enough clout to obliterate those who have been a blessing to him. **The spirit of rebellion not only leads assistant pastors to defect, but it inspires them to fight against the authorities that have been set over them.**

Absalom fought against his own father and failed. Judas tried to destroy Jesus his teacher and Lord, but that is the mother of all deceptions. You cannot destroy the Lord through your uprising. Lucifer thought he could dethrone God, but that was also not possible. What folly! What unthinkable madness!

### He Threatened to Destroy His Own Father

Some years ago, I sat at home fellowshipping with a Nigerian minister. This pastor friend of mine is the overseer of several large churches scattered all over Nigeria. As we chatted, I realized he had had experiences similar to mine. He spoke of one mutinous pastor who had grown up in his house as something of a servant.

### I Will Publish a Book about You

This young man had graduated into becoming the pastor of one of his largest branch churches. My friend told me that this pastor had become anarchistic and fought against him. I was struck by one of the comments he made.

He told me, "This young man rebelled, broke away and began to say all sorts of malicious things about me."

His own son in the ministry said, "I will publish a book of seditious material that will bring you down."

### I Will Run You out of This Town

How interesting, I thought. I remembered a similar threat I had received from a rebel pastor. That person had said he was going to run me out of my own city.

You see, this is the mother of all deceptions. This is the spirit of *Absalom* that *fights against your own father*. The spirit of *Lucifer* is the spirit that tries to *replace and take over* rightful authority. The spirit of *Judas* is the treacherous spirit that *betrays and turns against* its own teacher.

I want you to grasp deeply right here that all of these things are impossible. You cannot replace God. And you cannot succeed in fighting your own father. God will not help you and in fact, He will fight against you. All of nature, including the wild ravens and eagles of the air, will fight against you. The Bible says,

> *The eye that mocketh at his father… the ravens of the valley*
> *shall pick it out, and the young eagles shall eat it.*
> PROVERBS 30:17

## STAGE SEVEN

### OPEN REBELLION

This is the stage where deceived insurrectionists fight openly against authority. This is fueled by the confidence a rebel develops over the months and years. He gains psychological support by gaining the support of some of the people he talked to. Remember that Lucifer gained the support of over a third of the angels. He has had time to analyze the merits and demerits of the person against whom he is rebelling. Then suddenly, he exposes himself to be what he is at heart.

**1. Lucifer did this.**

> *And there was war in heaven …and the dragon [the devil]*
> *fought…* REVELATION 12:7

**2. Absalom fought against his father.**

> *And David said… Behold, my son (Absalom), which came*
> *forth of my bowels, seeketh my life…* 2 SAMUEL 16:11

**3. Absalom tried to become his father in all aspects, including in the bedroom.**

*...and Absalom went in unto his father's concubines in the sight of all Israel.*   2 SAMUEL 16:22

**4. Judas betrayed and fought against his Lord and master.**

*...Judas... came, and with him a great multitude with swords... Now he that betrayed him gave them a sign, saying, Whomsoever I shall kiss, that same is he: hold him fast.*
MATTHEW 26:47, 48

Judas had told them to get a good hold of Christ and not let him go. This is the open fight against your master, teacher or your father. It is what I call the open rebellion stage of disloyalty. This brings us to the last and final stage of this drama. It is what I call the execution stage.

## STAGE EIGHT: EXECUTION

All rebels come to the same end -- execution. Rebellion is an essentially evil thing. The Bible teaches us that rebellion is as witchcraft.

*For rebellion is as the sin of witchcraft...*   1 SAMUEL 15:23

The Biblical punishment for witchcraft is execution.

*Thou shalt not suffer a witch to live.*   EXODUS 22:18

God does not support rebellion in any form or fashion. Do not involve yourself in any kind of rebellion. Those who get involved in revolts are often simple-minded people. Many of them do not understand the seriousness of what is afoot.

*And with Absalom went two hundred men out of Jerusalem, that were called; and they went in their simplicity, and they knew not any thing.*   2 SAMUEL 15:11

Because of their innocence and ignorance, many people fall into rebellion. If Absalom's followers had known exactly what they were doing, I believe they would not have followed him.

The fruit of rebellion throughout the Bible is very clear -- execution. God will divinely displace and replace you with someone else. Your seat will be taken by another who is worthier than you. You will be banished into obscurity and oblivion. There will be a curse on you and your family. Just study the following list of executions:

### Lucifer

> *And the great dragon was cast out, that old serpent, called the Devil, and Satan, which deceiveth the whole world: he was cast out into the earth, and his angels were cast out with him.*
> REVELATION 12:9

### Absalom

> *And ten young men... compassed about and smote Absalom, and slew him.* 2 SAMUEL 18:15

### Ahithophel

> *...Ahithophel... hanged himself, and died...* 2 SAMUEL 17:23

### Shemei

> *So the king commanded Benaiah... which went out, and fell upon him (Shemei), that he died...* 1 KINGS 2:46

### Adonijah

> *And King Solomon sent by the hand of Benaiah the son of Jehoiada; and he fell upon him (Adonijah) that he died.*
> 1 KINGS 2:25

# Judas

*And he (Judas)… went and hanged himself.*   MATTHEW 27:5

# Slipping Into Disloyalty

*(For reasons of privacy you may want to make notes on a photocopy of this page.)*

## Chapter Two - My Action Plan:

1. Who in my church or organization is, or could be, slipping into disloyalty?

2. What stage(s) of disloyalty need my further thought (agreement/disagreement)? Why?

    A. The Independent Spirit

    B. Offense

    C. Passivity

    D. The Critical Stage

    E. The Political Stage

    F. Deception

    G. Open Rebellion

    H. Execution

3. Did I see myself described in any of these stages of disloyalty?

4. Who comes to mind that I need to . . .

    A. Share or discuss this chapter with? Why?

    B. Confront about disloyalty issues? When?

# CHAPTER 3

# A Culture of Allegiance

Culture can simply be defined as "the way we think and the way we do things around here." The culture of a church is a very powerful force. A church can display either a culture of loyalty or disloyalty. In visiting different churches, I have noticed a prevailing climate of either loyalty or treachery.

Once, when I was in South Africa to minister, I interacted with several assistant pastors and leaders. Throughout those exchanges, I noticed a certain reverence and genuine love that all the associates seemed to have for their senior pastor. Never once was there a sarcastic remark from anyone. They seemed to sincerely love and respect their pastor.

## That Church Had a Culture of Disloyalty

I recall also being in another church where the contrast was unmistakable. I found assistant pastors who did not hesitate to make sarcastic comments about their head pastor behind his back. They seemed to think that they were gaining my sympathy by applauding aspects of my church while maintaining an unfavorable picture of their own church.

I remember one of the pastors said, "Oh, I like your church building. It's simple and practical."

And he continued, "You know our 'man' (he was referring to his senior pastor). We have been doing this expensive project for many years, and we are getting nowhere."

I just looked on in amazement! You see, by this comment this pastor had ridiculed his senior pastor and that pastor's management in front of me, an outsider.

I remember another time when I was officiating at the wedding of a church member. The bride was from my church, and the bridegroom was from another church. I had asked my associate to perform the nuptial ceremony so that I would preach.

### He Said, "I Like Your Style"

After the service, this pastor who belonged to the bridegroom's church approached me and said, "I am very happy to meet you. I like your style."

He added, "I'm glad to meet a Bishop who allows his associates to participate in the ceremony. You know, at our place things are different. Our man, the Bishop, would not have allowed anybody else to play a prominent role."

I listened quietly and thought to myself, "This man thinks he's praising me by making cynical remarks about his Bishop."

### But He Was a Rebel

I said to myself, "This is a rebel in the making." And sure enough, a year later, this pastor rebelled against his Bishop.

I am talking about a culture of disloyalty. A culture you remember can simply be defined as "the way we think and the way we do things around here." A church's culture is simply the set of customs and values that the members are accustomed to.

The culture of a church is a very powerful force. You may not be aware of it, or ignore it, but it is real. An effective leader gives priority to developing a good culture of faithfulness, fidelity and loyalty. Even in the business world, the culture of the company determines how well it performs.

In my church, we have gradually developed what I call a culture of loyalty. It is unacceptable to speak negatively about any minister. I myself make no sarcastic remarks about my friends and pastors behind their backs. If I have anything to say, I will usually just say it.

### People Notice Loyalty

Lighthouse church members will brand you a rebel if you began to speak in a certain way. One brother, coming from a less loyal church culture, remarked, "Your church is air tight." What he was trying to say was that he had found our culture impermeable to all forms of malicious talk. As a result, the undercurrents of murmuring and discontented people are not free to exist in our environment.

## FIVE KEYS TO SHAPING A CULTURE OF LOYALTY

### 1. The Key of the North Wind

*The north wind driveth away rain: so doth an angry countenance a backbiting tongue.* PROVERBS 25:23

This first key to developing a culture of loyalty may come as a surprise. It is what I call the Key of the North Wind. The Bible says that the north wind drives away the rain. A powerful rainstorm is driven away by a strong wind. In the same way, the power of malicious backbiting tongues can be neutralized by certain facial expressions.

### Your Face Is the North Wind

Just show someone by your facial expression that you are not interested in his or her conversation. According to the Bible, your disagreeable attitude is strong enough to deter unruly and rebellious elements. People will gradually get to know that disloyal people are not welcome there.

One day a certain young lady came to see one of my associate pastors. She mistakenly thought she was praising him when she said, "How approachable you are!"

She went on, "If it wasn't for you, I would have left this church."

My associate pastor told me, "As soon as she made that remark, I 'squeezed' my face."

(In other words, this young lady was saying that I was not a nice enough pastor. And the only reason she could give for staying on as a member was the presence of my associate.)

However, the expression on the associate pastor's face was enough to quench any further traitorous discussion. You see, the pastor could have thought that he was very anointed and that this was why a church member was saying what she said. But that would have been a mistake.

Assistant pastors must not be deceived by the temptation to be disloyal. The devil often uses ordinary people to bring about these temptations. The women in Israel sang, "Saul has killed his thousands, and David his tens of thousands." This was not true. David had just killed Goliath and not tens of thousands of Philistines. Do not be deceived by empty words out of the mouths of baby Christians.

### The Friendly Assistant Pastor

Often the assistant pastor seems friendlier than the head pastor. This is because the senior pastor may have duties that are for the benefit of the whole church, while important but lesser needs of the church are delegated to the assistant pastor to handle. The assistant pastor therefore can be more approachable and can seem accessible.

Some associates are deceived into thinking that the congregation prefers them to the senior minister. A loyal assistant must learn to tamp down all gossip, backbiting and criticism of the senior pastor and others in leadership.

### Her Face Frightened Me

Many years ago, I attended a meeting of a church group to which I belonged. At the close of the service, the pastor decided to take a second offering. When he announced it, I immediately turned to the person sitting by me and murmured, "Why take a second offering? It's not necessary." **She said nothing but gave me a look I will never forget.**

Suddenly my conscience condemned me and I realized I had done something wrong. I felt so bad that I had complained, even though it was unknown to the pastor.

*...an angry countenance [drives away] a backbiting tongue.*
PROVERBS 25:23

## 2. The key of constant pruning

To have a culture of loyalty you must constantly root out disloyal elements that find their way into your midst. I believe that no one should stay on in a church when he or she does not want to. I have discovered that if anyone indicates his desire to resign, it is best for such a person not to stay on but to leave immediately. This is because his heart has already left the church.

### Remove Disloyal People Quickly

I learned this lesson the hard way when I encouraged a rebellious pastor to stay on after he had indicated his desire to leave. The extra months he remained were not worth the trouble they yielded. Now, I have a different policy. If you indicate your desire to leave, you will have to go immediately. Even if you change your mind, it will be too late. The reason for this is simple,

*...a little leaven leaveneth the whole lump?*
1 CORINTHIANS 5:6

One dissenting employee pollutes the others with his disgruntled attitude. After Judas resigned from Jesus' ministry, Jesus told him,

*...That thou doest, do quickly.* JOHN 13:27

One pastor of a large church described how many unhappy experiences he underwent because he retained a pastor who did not want to stay on. People who don't want to be with you must go; and they must leave as soon as possible. It's as simple as that.

Some pastors are so soft that they do not remove openly rebellious elements. I remember the testimony of a pastor who graduated from the Bible school of a church with a disloyal culture.

He said, "It was obvious that the Dean and lecturers of this Bible school had little confidence in their own church." "They could rarely find something positive to say about their church."

Then this pastor said something that I find amazing! He said, "Whenever there was need of an example to illustrate a negative point, they would choose their own church as the example."

He went on, "Once, when we were being lectured on administration and management, the lecturer said, 'See, this church (and its pastor of course) is an example of a church with a poor administration and bad management.'"

What do you think the students thought about every time the senior pastor taught in the Bible school? Such devious, undisciplined people need to be weeded out of the system. Do not allow any leader to pollute your precious sheep.

### 3. The key of creating fire

At times it is necessary to create conditions that expose disloyal elements within the team.

> *...there came a viper out of the heat...* ACTS 28:3

When Paul came ashore soaking wet on the island of Melita, the local folk graciously kindled a fire to warm him and his companions. Paul gathered some sticks and laid them on the fire.

### The Stick Was a Snake

Suddenly, a viper (which is, by the way, one of the most dangerous species of snakes) came out of the fire and fastened itself to Paul's hand. One of the 'sticks' was a snake! The fire exposed it. Before being subjected to fire, some snakes can pose as ordinary sticks.

What fire am I talking about? The fire of *time*, for instance, is an example of something that exposes the snake-like nature of some people. **Difficult times and hardships bring out the true nature of people.** Sometimes softening the path an associate minister or any of the others in church leadership travel does not help to test their hearts.

Jesus suffered in the ministry from wicked people all around him. We must also suffer. And suffering brings out the true nature in people.

### Do Not Be under Pressure to Promote People

Do not be in a hurry to promote people. If they will rebel because they have not been promoted, they will rebel even if they are promoted. Should you not believe me, just try it out! I have come to see that rebellion is a matter of the heart. If a person will cause trouble, no amount of money or attractive conditions of service will prevent it.

### Transfer and See What Happens

One of the fires that can bring out snakes within a large denomination of churches or any organization is the "fire of transfer." Numerous pastors when subjected to the possibility of transfer rebel against the authority. Why should you rebel against your transfer? Did you obey the call of God on condition that you would live in a rich city? A person's reaction to being transferred reveals a lot about his character.

## 4. The key of working only with willing people

Make sure you do not have unwilling (trapped) people around you. Constantly make a way for them to leave if they want to. One thing you should not have is someone who wants to leave, but because of financial or other reasons feels trapped within your organization. The hearts of such people are not with you anymore. They can become traitors. **Make a way for such people to exit peacefully.**

There is nothing like working with a willing and happy person.

*For if there be first a willing mind...* 2 CORINTHIANS 8:12

I have decided to assist the departure of any unwilling person who wants to leave. Because in helping them I will also be helping myself.

## 5. The key of teaching against disloyalty

Constant teaching on the subjects of loyalty and disloyalty is very important. Most people are ignorant of the evolvement of the disloyalty process. In other words, many rebels are unaware of what they are doing. Constant education will prevent people from unknowingly involving themselves in traitorous activities.

Anyone who wants to build a large church must constantly teach on faithfulness and loyalty. No one is born instinctually faithful and loyal. Every minister or leader will have his share of temptations to disloyalty. The leaders under you or in your organization will develop a culture of loyalty as you constantly teach about it and lead by example.

# A Culture of Allegiance

*(For reasons of privacy you may want to make notes on a photocopy of this page.)*

## Chapter Three - My Action Plan:

1. In a few words, how would I characterize the role of and/or commitment to allegiance in my church, denomination or organization?

2. In my spiritual leadership structure:
   a. Who understands and supports the priority of allegiance? How?

   b. Who seems not to value or support allegiance? Why?

   c. Is the principle of allegiance/loyalty misunderstood or abused? Cite an example.

3. Which of the five keys to creating a culture of loyalty am I using or do I need to use?
   a. The key of the North Wind                    *Using*    *Need to use*

   b. The key of constant pruning                   *Using*    *Need to use*

   c. The key of creating fire                      *Using*    *Need to use*

   d. The key of working only with willing people   *Using*    *Need to use*

   e. The key of teaching against disloyalty        *Using*    *Need to use*

## CHAPTER 4

# Seven Truths About Loyalty

## TRUTH ONE: LOYALTY DEMANDS FULL PERSUASION

To lead effectively, you must be fully convinced in your heart about what you are involved in. And to be a committed member of a ministry team requires what I call **full persuasion**.

If I expect you to be loyal to me, you have to be sure about me. Am I someone you can trust? Am I who I claim to be? I once asked some pastors, "What will make people stop talking about me?"

One person gave the right answer. She said, "If you stop doing the work of the ministry, people will stop talking about you!" And that is very true.

### Jesus Was Accused

In Luke 23:2, Jesus was accused by many people of,

> ...*misleading our people...* TwentieTH CenTury New
> TesTament

> *...teaching our people sedition...* THE FOUR GOSPELS (E.V. RIEU)

> *...preventing them from paying taxes to the Emperor...* TWENTIETH CENTURY NEW TESTAMENT

> *...telling them that it is wrong to pay taxes...* NEW TESTAMENT IN MODERN ENGLISH

> *...claiming to be an anointed king...* EMPHASIZED NEW TESTAMENT

And in Luke 11:15, Jesus was accused of being able to cast out devils because he is,

> *...in league with Beelzebub, the chief of the evil spirits...* THE NEW TESTAMENT IN MODERN ENGLISH

## Paul Was Accused

In Acts 24:5, Paul was accused of being

> *...a source of mischief...* NEW TESTAMENT IN MODERN SPEECH

> *...a veritable plague...* BERKELEY VERSION OF THE NEW TESTAMENT

> *...a public pest...* TWENTIETH CENTURY NEW TESTAMENT

> *...a disturber of the peace...* WEYMOUTH TRANSLATION

> *...one who stirs up disputes...* TWENTIETH CENTURY NEW TESTAMENT

*...a fomenter of discord...* NEW ENGLISH BIBLE

*...a ringleader of the sect...* KING JAMES VERSION

In Acts 24:6, he was also accused of being someone who

*...also attempted to desecrate even the temple...* THE EMPHA-
SIZED NEW TESTAMENT

*...was attempting to make the temple unclean...*
NEW TESTAMENT IN BASIC ENGLISH

Anyone working with Paul would have to be fully persuaded about his true character. Was he really the ringleader of a sect and the source of mischief? Did he ever attempt to desecrate the temple? I wouldn't like to work with person who was as evil as that. It is important to establish in your heart all the facts about the ministry or person with whom you're working. Be fully persuaded so that when accusations, trials and testings come, you will be able to remain faithful.

### Can There Be Smoke Without Fire?
As the adage goes, "Where there is smoke there is fire." In other words, there is some truth in every rumor. But the obligation of believers is to find out the real truth behind every rumor. Is there any truth in these terrible accusations? The answer is no.

You see, in the normal experience of ministry, there will be regular accusations, rumors and stories about every man of God.

### All Pastors Will Be Accused
I remember visiting a pastor who had been accused of committing adultery with some of his church members. A popular newspaper published this scandalous story. I decided to visit that church on a Sunday morning to encourage him. That day, as I interacted with some of the other pastors and loyal members, I realized that there were probably questions in their minds. I knew immediately that they would have to be fully persuaded about their pastor.

You see it was a matter of his word against the accuser's word. Who was telling the truth -- the accuser or the pastor? If you decide to stay on, you must be prepared to confidently defend the integrity of the ministry.

> *...I am not ashamed: for I know whom I have believed, and am persuaded...* 2 TIMOTHY 1:12

Do not stay on in a ministry if you have lots of questions in your mind. Answer the questions for yourself or leave.

### Openness Breeds Full Persuasion

### 1. Be Open about finances

Let those who matter know the source of everything you have. Do not be a mystery personality. Some pastors when asked, "How did you get this expensive car?" Respond by saying, "The Lord has provided."

We know that the Lord has provided, but how did He provide it and through whom?

Even if people fail to question you, be it known unto you, that they are asking those questions in their minds. Although I am under no obligation to do so, I try to explain to those with whom I work closely the source of all my blessings. I want them to be fully persuaded as to what I really am.

I don't believe in being a mystery person. **When people start accusing, it is those around you who must be able to respond confidently and correctly.**

### 2. Be Open about your vision

Help people understand what you are trying to achieve. Let them know why you are so zealous about your vision. This is one of the reasons I teach by giving long lists of reasons why certain things should be done.

I once taught, "Twenty Reasons Why You Should Be a Permanent Member of a Church." I also remember teaching, "Fifty-Four Reasons Why You Should Be a Soul Winner." When you give 50 reasons for doing something, don't you think he the person would be fully persuaded?

### They Thought He Was on Vacation

I recall one pastor who was committing so many misdeeds that he had to be corrected and even suspended. To preserve this pastor's ministry, I kept the details very private, and the congregation even thought his suspension was a vacation.

However, when this rebellious pastor eventually defected from my ministry he began spreading all sorts of stories about me. You see, he had to justify his unexpected defection. But nobody knew that this pastor was undergoing disciplinary measures because of his multiple wrongdoings.

### Now, I Was under Fire!

However, when all sorts of questions arose concerning this man's character, I had a hard time explaining to people what was going on. Ironically, my church members were now questioning my integrity. This was a great lesson to me! Sometimes it is good to explain certain issues as they develop. Openness about what is going on generates confidence, understanding and the fullest assurance, especially in a crisis.

*He that is not with me is against me...* MATTHEW 12:30

**You cannot be neutral in a crisis.** You must know about the issue and face the issue. You must know what you stand for, and you must be prepared to die for it. I don't want to work with anyone who is "neutral." Either you believe in what is going on, or you are against it.

Dear Christian friend, be fully persuaded that you are in a good church where God wants you to be. Be fully persuaded about the pastor in charge. Before you venture into full-time ministry, be fully persuaded about it. This is absolutely essential for the development of true loyalty.

## TRUTH TWO: YOUR LOYALTY MUST BE TO THE HIGHER AUTHORITY

In a large organization like the church, there will always be a number of different authorities you must submit to. Some will have a higher rank than others. The lesson here is **when the question of loyalty arises, your**

**loyalty must be to the higher authority.**

For example, the structure in our ministry consists of Fellowship Shepherds, Ministry Shepherds, Branch or Chapel Pastors and Senior Ministers.

If, for instance, the Branch Pastor begins to say things that are contrary to the general vision of the church, your loyalty must go to the higher authority. But, if the most Senior Pastor begins to say or do things that are contrary to Christ, you are not supposed to follow him. Even Apostle Paul said,

> *Follow my example, as I follow the example of Christ.*
> 1 CORINTHIANS 11:1 (NIV)

In other words, Paul was saying, follow me only as long as I follow Christ. The day I stop following Christ is the day you must stop following me. Your loyalty in this case is to the higher authority -- that is Christ. I am convinced that many people do not understand this principle.

### Whom Must I Follow?

Many years ago, when Jim Jones led hundreds of people to commit suicide, the whole world was stunned. Since then, people have tried to put many genuine pastors in the category of Jim Jones. With this in mind, let me tell you how to distinguish a genuine minister of Christ from a heretic.

A genuine minister will always tell you, "Do not follow me if I am not following Christ." (Christ would never tell you to drink cyanide. If your pastor is telling you to drink cyanide, it is certainly wrong.) I always tell church members that because I am a man, I can make mistakes. Therefore, follow me only as I follow Christ.

### The Pastor Stole the Church

I remember one charismatic denomination that had a large branch church in a city in Ghana. One day, the Branch Pastor had a conflict with the General Overseer of that denomination. Following the dispute, he decided to take control of the branch church and change its name. Would you believe it? This man painted over the original name of the church and put up a new signboard with a new name. He then announced to the church that the assembly was no longer a member of their former denomination. This defecting pastor stole the church building, church property, church instruments and even the pulpit.

However, many of the members knew that their loyalty was to the higher authority, which in this case was the General Overseer. They said, "We are not going to be a part of this rebellion. If you decide to rebel and steal a whole church, we will not follow you! Our loyalty is to our General Overseer."

I am sad to tell you, however, that many of the church members followed this renegade minister. These things can only happen because people have not been taught the principles of loyalty.

## TRUTH THREE: A LOYAL PERSON DOES NOT WITHHOLD INFORMATION

A loyal person is open to his senior about whatever is going on. I consider someone loyal if he tells me about any corruption that is taking place. If I find out that he knew all along, but said nothing, I will consider him to be disloyal.

There are several examples in the Bible of people not withholding information. Some of these led to great revelations and blessings.

The Apostle Paul wrote to the Corinthians and said,

> *It is reported commonly that there is fornication among you...*
> 1 CORINTHIANS 5:1

Notice that Paul did not receive a word of knowledge about the extent of immorality going on in the church. Someone reported it to him. **A good and loyal structure works: faithful people inform the top leaders about anything that is out of order.** We would not have the teachings of 1 Corinthians 5 if someone had not reported about this act of sin.

Observe how another family reported to Paul some happenings in the church. This report did not even come from the pastor, but from an ordinary church member named Chloe.

*For it hath been declared unto me of...the house of Chloe, that*
*there are contentions...* 1 CORINTHIANS 1:11

Such reporting leads to the edifying of the church. There is a real difference between godly reporting to the appropriate authorities and slanderous gossip.

### The Pastor's Fiancé Had Another Boyfriend

I remember a minister who proposed to marry a young lady and began courting her. Unknown to him, this girl, although a regular member of the church, had an unbeliever for a boyfriend on the side. The minister did not know what he was dealing with!

There happened to be another church member who worked in the same area as this young lady. After awhile this sister said to herself, "This young lady is preparing to marry one of our pastors. But I see that she has an unbeliever boyfriend on the side. She is leading a double life."

### The Beans Are Spilled

This sister mustered up her courage, went to the office of the church and "spilled the beans." The rest of the pastors were horrified but thankful to this loyal sister. You see, godly reporting saved that pastor's life.

If you do not withhold information, it may save your life some day. For example, Mordecai was sentenced to death through the evil conspiracy of Haman. Just before he was to be executed, it was discovered that much earlier, Mordecai had exposed two killers who almost murdered the king.

*...Bigthan and Teresh... ...sought to lay hand on the king*
*Ahasuerus. And the thing was known to Mordecai, who told*
*it...* ESTHER 2:21, 22

When you know of something evil, you are expected to reveal it to the appropriate authority! Mordecai's act of loyalty was recorded in the annals of the nation. The king could not sleep one night and was reading some materials from the archives. **He discovered that Mordecai (whom he was about to execute) had, in fact, saved his life.**

This revelation proved that Mordecai was actually a very loyal person.

When you withhold information, the impression is given that you are in support of what is going on. We call this complicity. If you uncover an insurrection and arrest all the rebels, that is the first step. The next thing is to find out all of those who knew about it.

Godly reporting can save the life of a church.

## TRUTH FOUR: LOYALTY IS BASED ON PRINCIPLES, NOT EMOTIONS

Many people operate by feelings and emotions rather than by a set of principles. Decisions based on emotions rather than principles are not substantial. If you have decided to belong to something, you must make your decision based on your principles and not on your feelings.

### They Said, "We Feel Sorry for Him"

Once upon a time, a dissident pastor went off on a tangent and decided to do the wrong thing. Some church members decided to follow him. When asked why they were following this renegade fellow, they answered, "We know what he is doing is wrong, but we feel sorry for him."

I have experienced rebellion before. Many people who follow rebels do so without thinking. Remember that all those who followed Absalom without seriously considering what they were doing were killed. Remember that the many angels who followed Lucifer were cast down. You must remember that when Korah the rebel was perishing, he was destroyed with his entire family and 300 others.

All of these people wouldn't have been destroyed had they thought twice about what they were doing. How could you follow somebody like Absalom, who was fighting his own father? Perhaps Absalom's good looks and long hair swayed the masses. The point I'm making is that loyalty must be based on principles and not feelings and emotions.

### The Return of the Rebel

Once, I had a pastor who left me with a small group of rebellious people. A few weeks later, I was informed that one of the rebels wanted to meet with me.

I was told that Rebel #2 wanted to meet with me. I responded, "Why should he want to meet with me. I have nothing to do with him anymore."

However, they insisted, "Please come down, he wants to talk with you." I agreed.

At the meeting I asked, "Young man, what can I do for you?"

"I have come to apologize for rebelling against you," he replied. "You have done me no wrong, and I don't see why I behaved the way I did."

So I asked him, "Why did you join Rebel #1 in fighting against me?"

### I Don't Know Why I Did It

He bowed his head and replied, "I don't know why."

He went on, "I was born again here. I grew up here. Everything I know in the Lord, I learned from you."

So I asked again, "Why did you do it?"

He shook his head and answered, "Pastor, I don't know why I did it."

This young man admitted that he acted out of emotion. He could not even explain to himself why he had taken the course of action that he took. Many disloyal people just follow the crowd. They feel that they are onto something new.

There was a pastor of a church who felt he was popular and broke away with a section of the church. This caused much pain for the senior pastor-in-charge and virtually destroyed the ministry. Those that joined the rebellion were initially very happy, thinking that they were on to something new and exciting.

### You Can't Fool Me Twice

After a year or so, this traitorous pastor travelled to America and never returned. He abandoned his breakaway church when the door opened for him to go to America. Those who followed him were very surprised and felt let down. (But what else can you expect from a rebel?)

It happened that some members of this now pastor-less group drifted over to join the Lighthouse Cathedral. Not long after, we also had an experience of rebellion. A rebellious pastor approached some of these new members and invited them to his renegade church.

One of the people he invited told us about the response he gave.

He said to this rebel pastor, "I once followed a pastor who did exactly what you are doing. I have seen all of this before. No one can fool me twice. There is no way that I am going to follow you!"

Church, let us stop playing games. Let us base our loyalty and commitment on principles and not on emotions. Baby Christians live by their feelings! Loyalty is broken when the Word and its principles are set aside.

Loyalty is to God and to his Word and to the principles of His Word.

### Jonathan Was Principled

Cast your mind back to Jonathan, the son of Saul. He realized that his father was wrong in principle. He also realized that his father was trying to murder an innocent young man. So he decided to help David even though it was emotionally difficult. Even though his actions were directed against his own family, it was the right thing to do.

Some people just follow family lines. If it's your brother or your sister, it must be right. Even if it is glaringly wrong. Jonathan was not like that. Look at what he said.

> ...but if it please my father to do thee evil, then I will shew it thee, and send thee away, that thou mayest go in peace...
> 1 SAMUEL 20:13

## TRUTH FIVE: LOYALTY WILL COST YOU RELATION-SHIPS AND FRIENDSHIPS

Everything has a price. Education has a price. Even your salvation has a price. The Bible says we are bought with a price. Loyalty also has a price.

To be loyal to someone means you cannot be loyal to everyone. Loyalty will cost you relationships and friendships. My loyalty to Christ has meant that I cannot maintain some of my old friendships.

### No Relationship is Meaningless

I have some friends with whom I can no longer flow. The reason for this is my loyalty to the Lord. I find it amazing that some Christians claim that they are simply friends with a rebellious person.

They say, "Oh, he's just a colleague from school."

I'll ask, "Are you sure?"

They answer, "Oh yes, it's just an old friendship. We never talk about church or anything like that."

I want you to meditate on the following verse. Please do not just brush it away.

> ...whosoever therefore will be a friend of the world is the enemy of God. JAMES 4:4

Notice that certain friendships are equivalent to enmity with God. No explanations are needed. Just the existence of the friendship implies enmity with God. Anyone who is the friend of my enemy is also my enemy.

You don't need to explain much about whether he's an old colleague, a social friend or a neighbor. The Bible says that the existence of certain friendships is equivalent to certain enmities.

You cannot take relationships for granted. They are not meaningless. They mean something. Every friendship or relationship will contribute something to your life.

I would advise every pastor, assistant pastor, elder, deacon, Bible study leader, committee chairman and every leader at any level in the church or any organization to observe the relationships and friendships that his associates maintain.

I once visited an assistant pastor friend of mine. As we chatted, he spent most of the time commending the achievements and accomplishments of another pastor (not his own senior pastor). He said virtually nothing about his own senior pastor or his own church. In fact, he seemed closer to this external pastor than he was to his own senior pastor.

### The Friendship That Didn't Pay

On my way home, I mused about the closeness that seemed to exist between this assistant and an external pastor. I thought to myself, "I wonder how long this assistant is going to be in his present ministry?"

Lo and behold, a few months later I heard the news that my assistant pastor friend had defected.

No relationship is meaningless. Friendship with this means enmity with that! Your commitment to a cause may even cost you your relationship with your family. Jesus said,

> *If any man come to me, and hate not his father, and mother,*
> *and wife, and children, and brethren, and sisters, yea, and his*
> *own life also, he cannot be my disciple.* LUKE 14:26

Certain things are virtually impossible to view openly. For instance, it is very rare to see two human beings having sex out in the open. Fornication is one thing you are unlikely to spot with your physical eyes. But the Bible says we should look diligently to see if there is any fornicator amongst us. How are we supposed to recognize fornicators?

The answer is obvious. You are supposed to look out for signs of it. For instance, when a couple that is not yet married visit each other until late after midnight.

It is the same thing with the concept of loyalty. Disloyalty is not easy to detect. You have to look for signs of it. And one of the signs is unhealthy friendships and relationships.

Your loyalty is revealed through the friends you keep. Some friendships will be broken if you are being loyal to Christ, to your church and to your pastor.

Jonathan's loyalty to David cost him his relationship with his own father.

> *And Jonathan answered Saul his father, and said unto him,*
> *Wherefore shall he be slain? what hath he done? And Saul cast*
> *a javelin at him...* 1 SAMUEL 20:32, 33

When Jonathan questioned the decision of his father to kill David, King Saul was so angry that he threw a spear at his son. Notice that Jonathan almost lost his life because of his loyalty to David. Loyalty is expensive.

## TRUTH SIX: LOYALTY MAY COST YOU PHYSICAL THINGS

The Bible teaches us that when Moses became a man, he had to choose between being loyal to God or to Pharaoh. His loyalty to God cost him everything. Moses may have become the next Prime Minister of Egypt. But his loyalty cost him his citizenship, his passport and his royal status. He lost it all because of Christ.

> *By faith Moses, when he was come to years, refused to be called the son of Pharaoh's daughter; Choosing rather to suffer afflic-tion with the people of God...* HEBREWS 11:24, 25

If someone is giving you money on a regular basis, and he rebels against God and against the church, you will have to choose between singing the praises of an Absalom and doing the right thing. If you decide to do what is principled, obviously your supply of cash will dry up. But, dear friend, that is the cost of loyalty.

## TRUTH SEVEN: LOYALTY DEMANDS ANALYSIS

Whenever your loyalty is tested, you will have to analyze several things to stay loyal. To analyze means to study and interpret the information set before you.

I want to show you a few things that you must analyze in order to stabilize your mind and your heart in what you are doing.

### 1. Analyze the Past

I want to show you how Paul appealed to Timothy to analyze things. First, he said analyze the past.

> *Wherefore I put thee in remembrance that thou stir up the gift of God, which is in thee by the putting on of my hands.*
> 2 TIMOTHY 1:6

Timothy was a man who was probably deviating from his call. Paul wrote to remind him of what had happened in the past. We don't know exactly what Paul was reminding Timothy about, but it must have related to his call. He said, "I'm reminding you of something."

Think about all that has happened in the past. How God called you and brought you to where you are. I always remember the stirrings and callings of the Spirit, which I began to feel very early in my life. I keep in mind the zeal and love I have always had for souls to be won. That helps me to remain loyal to the call of God upon my life.

I am certain that many people do not think for a moment about the past.

## I Found Someone with a Passion for Souls

I remember one of the first times I talked with my senior associate pastor. It was in a room in the medical hostel of the university. We spoke about preaching the gospel in the towns and villages of our nation. I realized he had the same passion and concern for souls that I had.

Something in my heart clicked, and I realized I had found someone I could work with. That discussion is still fresh in my mind. It helps me to stay on track and to do what I originally set out to do. That is why today we have a mass evangelism ministry. Anytime I want to do anything else, God reminds me of what he said to me earlier on.

I have also decided to remember past associations and friendships. Once, a rebellious character went out of his way to slander me to my friend.

## Beware of Pastor Dag

He said, "Be careful of Pastor Dag."

My friend replied, "Why are you telling me to be careful of him?"

He answered, "He is into the occult."

"What! You must be mad!" my loyal friend continued, "Do you know how long I have known Dag? You don't seem to know how long-standing our relationship is."

My loyal friend then pointed out to him, "There must be something wrong with you."

Anytime you analyze the events of the past, it will help you to remain loyal.

## 2. Analyze the Individual Concerned

In order to remain loyal over a long period of time, you will need to make a good analysis of the individual concerned. Paul said that Timothy should continue in the things that he had learned. Most importantly, Timothy should remember the type of person from whom he learned what he knows.

> *But continue thou in the things which thou hast learned and*
> *hast been assured of, knowing of whom thou hast learned them;*
> 2 TIMOTHY 3:14

When people begin to come up with all forms of seditious stories and slanderous reports, think carefully about what they are saying. Analyze the individual who is being criticized and whether it makes sense.

### Who Earns More:  Doctor or Pastor?

One time, someone said that I was preaching for money, trying to get rich quickly. This person obviously is not a deep thinker. If this individual were to analyze what he was saying, he would realize that very few people are privileged to be medical doctors. He would also realize that I must have been out of my mind to leave the practice of medicine in order to make money by collecting people's pennies.  How absurd!

It is much easier to make money as a medical doctor. This dishonest character is refusing to consider the financial status of my medical colleagues and how much money they are earning.

All I am saying is this: analyze the individual who is being criticized and it will help you to decide whether to be loyal or not.

> *But thou hast fully known my doctrine, manner of life, purpose,*
> *faith, longsuffering, charity, patience, Persecutions, afflictions…*
> 2 TIMOTHY 3:10, 11

Paul said, "You have known my lifestyle and my character."  He was appealing to Timothy to acknowledge how intimately he had known him. When I meet people I have heard unfavorable rumors about, I find them to be quite different from how they have been portrayed. Get to know the individual personally.  It is only then that you will know the true picture.

### Did the Pastor Go to the Nightclub?

A church member once told me that she had seen one of my pastors taking a lady into a nightclub. I thought about what this lady was saying for a moment, and then I dismissed it. Why did I dismiss that story as being frivolous? As I analyzed the person who was telling me the story and the pastor it concerned, I felt that her accusation was a ridiculous.

I've known the pastor in question for many years, and I have never had cause to doubt his integrity. Why should I listen to the tale of some silly personality whose agenda I'm not sure of? Of course, I would take an accusation like that more seriously if it came from more than one person.

> Against an elder receive not an accusation, but before two or three witnesses. 1 Timothy 5:19

Loyalty demands continuous analysis in the face of constant accusations, rumors and slanderous stories.

### I Supported Him Till...

Some years ago, a man of God I loved was accused of committing adultery with a member of his church. I had heard this pastor preaching and teaching many times and have been very moved by the gift of God upon his life. So when this rumor was confirmed, I wrote a letter to him, encouraging him.

I told him I was praying for and standing with him. I emphasized that I still believed in him, in spite of what had happened. I felt that I should still be loyal to him because he had probably made a terrible mistake of which he had repented.

### A Girl in the Hotel Room

Although many people criticized that pastor in the heat of the scandal, I constantly defended him, both in public and in private. You see, the Bible says the righteous man falls seven times and rises again. So I felt that he would rise again. However, a few years later, another event made me turn my loyalty away from this person.

I visited this minister at a hotel. I had a message for him. The receptionist showed me the room in which he was staying.

I went up to his door and knocked. Someone came to the door and opened it. It was a half-naked girl with a flimsy towel that she held up in front of her!

I was startled.

"Oh, is pastor in?" I asked.

"I have a message for him."

She smiled sweetly and said, "Yes. He's in bed."

I quickly sputtered out the message and left in a daze.

As I walked out of the hotel I asked myself, "What was this undressed young lady doing in this man of God's hotel room? Is this man not tired of scandals?"

I analyzed the situation. Years after the scandal, this pastor was still engaging himself in questionable and immoral behavior.

It was at this point in time that my loyalty to this individual ceased.

### 3. Analyze the Form of Words You Have Heard

*Hold fast the form of sound words, which thou hast heard of me...*   2 TIMOTHY 1:13

You are supposed to check on what pastors preach to you from the pulpit. Is it accurate? Is it the Word?

This will help you to know whether to remain loyal to them or not.

*These were more noble... and searched the scriptures daily...*
ACTS 17:11

You are also supposed to compare what they are preaching now to what they used to preach. This is because some start out with Bible-based preaching and end up with all sorts of weird doctrines. When it's not the Word of God anymore, you are supposed to "defect from the defector."

#### Is Your Pastor Preaching the Right Thing?

Some ministers have drifted off from the mainstream of Bible doctrines into extreme versions of some fundamental truths. There are great truths about the Holy Spirit, prayer, prosperity, etc. But all of these can be perverted and misinterpreted. God didn't say we would whistle in tongues or bark and bite people in the Spirit. But, in some places, these are being taught as biblical truths. Let's stay with the mainstream.

We have to analyze the type of messages that our man of God gives us. Has he been lying to us all along? Does he normally slander other people? Is he a talebearer? If you are suddenly hearing criticisms of someone you love and trust, analyze the sort of things he has said all along. He is likely to be saying the same sort of things. It will help you to decide whether to trust him or not. Remember this little phrase, **He who lies to you about others will lie to others about you.** Lying is usually a chronic disease.

### He Preached His Opinion

Do I usually preach my opinion? Or do I preach the Word?

I was once at a meeting with a group of pastors in my city. One of them said, "When we preach in our churches on Sunday mornings, we usually give our opinions."

I asked, "Did you say you preach your opinion?"

"Yes, we all preach our opinions," he insisted.

I challenged him right there, "We are supposed to preach the Word of God and not our opinions."

You see there is a difference between your opinion and the Word of God. Do not just accept what anybody says because of who he is.

### Some Preachers Are Clever

Some preachers are clever with words. The Bible says they sway the hearts of the simple with their nice sounding maxims. **Don't let them get away with their clever little phrases.** Take them up on what they say! Anything that they say must be consistent with the written Word. If it doesn't correspond to the Word, then it is unacceptable.

Analyze the form of words you are receiving – are they somebody's opinion or the Word?

I am trying to grow a beautiful lawn in my house, but I am having lots of problems with weeds. It is difficult to see the difference between the real grass and the weeds. The weeds seem to grow faster. They are more flamboyant and flashy. **But the good gardener analyzes the difference,**

**pulls out the weeds and waters the good grass.**

### 4. Analyze the Word of God

Once upon a time, I had to tell my church members to mark and avoid a stubbornly perverse and rebellious individual in the church. Some people were surprised that I had given such an instruction.

### We Marked the Rebel

They asked, "How can you ask us to stay away from a brother?" Once again, these were people who do not read their Bibles. The Word of God says,

> *...mark them which cause divisions and offenses... and avoid them.* ROMANS 16:17

All through the Scriptures, you will find the historical records of Lucifer, the rebel; Absalom, the papa killer; and Adonijah, the usurper.

Ahitophel, the traitor; Shemei, who cursed King David; and Judas, who betrayed Jesus, are just a few more examples of treacherous people. Can we not expect to see these same people in real church life?

The Bible is a practical book and it declares,

> *The thing that hath been, it is that which shall be...* ECCLESIASTES 1:9

Read your Bible and analyze what it is saying. You will realize that we are experiencing nothing unusual.

### Did Jesus Make a Mistake?

How could Jesus choose a team of pastors only for one of them to become a traitor? **When Jesus chose leaders, one of them turned out to be a devil. Do not be surprised if one of your leaders turns out to be a villain.** Someone may question Jesus' ability to choose leaders. Jesus tried to choose the best, but look at what happened. If you appoint pastors and one of them turns against you, remember that the same thing happened to Christ.

> *The disciple is not above his master...* LUKE 6:40

# Seven Truths About Loyalty

*(For reasons of privacy you may want to make notes on a photocopy of this page.)*

## Chapter Four - My Action Plan:

In my leadership roles, which of the seven truths have I experienced or witnessed in action?

1) ☐ Loyalty Demands Full Persuasion
   a) Who?,     When?,     Where?
   b) The outcome and lesson learned?

2) ☐ Your Loyalty Must Be to the Higher Authority
   a) Who?,     When?,     Where?
   b) The outcome and lesson learned?

3) ☐ A Loyal Person Does Not Withhold Information
   a) Who?,     When?,     Where?
   b) The outcome and lesson learned?

4) ☐ Loyalty Is Based on Principles, Not Emotions
   a) Who?,     When?,     Where?
   b) The outcome and lesson learned?

5) ☐ Loyalty Will Cost You Relationships and Friendships
   a) Who?,     When?,     Where?
   b) The outcome and lesson learned?

6) ☐ Loyalty May Cost You Physical Things
   a) Who?,     When?,     Where?
   b) The outcome and lesson learned?

7) ☐ Loyalty Demands Analysis
   a) Who?,     When?,     Where?
   b) The outcome and lesson learned?

# CHAPTER 5

# Signs of Disloyalty

I learned some time ago that leaders often do not know their flock as they truly are. If you are a leader, people will pretend before you all the time. They will conceal their shortcomings from you and only tell you things they believe you want to hear. They will praise you because they know you like the encouragement.

When someone you relate with becomes disloyal, do not expect that person to announce, "I no longer support you." Every good leader must watch out for what I call the "Signs of Disloyalty."

### Leaders: Watch for the Signs

These signs will help you navigate through the maze of people who sing your praises. When those surrounding Christ seemed to praise him and acknowledge him as a great leader, Jesus did not trust himself to them.

> *But Jesus did not commit himself unto them, because he knew all men, And needed not that any should testify of man: for he knew what was in man.* JOHN 2:24, 25

Every good leader must not subject himself to men. Neither should he trust what people are saying, wholeheartedly. You'll recall that when Jesus entered Jerusalem on Palm Sunday, he was hailed and praised.

### Don't Trust Everyone

In a certain sense, you must learn to take everything with a grain of salt. In another part of the Bible, Jesus' own brothers suggested that he go public with his ministry.

> *His brethren therefore said unto him, Depart hence, and go into*
> *Judea that thy disciples also may see the works that thou doest.*
> JOHN 7:3

They encouraged him, explaining that no one who wanted to have a far-reaching ministry should keep himself in secret. Remember, these were Jesus' own brethren. Jesus simply answered and said, "My time is not yet come." But in John 7:5, the Bible reveals that this advice coming from his own brothers was not genuine.

> *For neither did his brethren believe in him.* JOHN 7:5

You can see right here that a leader is often subjected to hypocritical advice and lying praises. This is the reason why every good leader must learn what I call the "Signs of Disloyalty."

The following are some of the signs people exhibit when they are disloyal or *potentially* disloyal.

### 1. A leader who disappoints you in times of pressure or crisis

Take notice of leaders who are missing when the church is going through difficult times. Watch out for people who are absent during hard times. It is in times of pressure that the true character of a person is revealed. In the heat of events, you may have to rebuke someone sharply, or you may have to overburden those you work with. Watch how they behave during such times; it will tell you something about their loyalty.

It is expected that everyone will cooperate in times of crisis. Some time ago, we had a crisis in our church relating to factions within our community. One day, in the heat of events, we had to go and see some officials in the government. When we went to see them, they explained that they wanted to see if we had any local support from people the community.

### The Three Deserters

I said, "Oh, that's not a problem; we have members of the community in our church. I even have community members working in our office."

So I left a hurried message for some of the church workers (who were also pastoral trainees) to join me in visiting these government officials. I wanted the government officials to see that we had genuine support from the community. Would you believe that these pastoral trainees did not turn up? They did not go to see the government officials in support of the church. I felt really depressed and let down in a time of crisis.

Afterward, I confronted the three deserters.

### Two Apologized

Shortly after this, two of them apologized for letting me down. But, the third rendered no such apology. I decided to say nothing, but just to watch him. I realized that I had detected a lack of full commitment. I was not surprised when a few weeks later I received a letter on my desk from this same brother. I can always tell when a letter is a resignation letter.

### I Resign

This letter had only one sentence, "I resign from your organization." I never saw this brother again and was not interested in seeing him anymore. Watch out for those who desert you in times of trouble. They are probably not loyal to you.

Why did Paul say he wouldn't work with Rev. John Mark? It was because John Mark had deserted him in a time of crisis.

> But Paul thought not good to take him [John Mark] with them, who departed [deserted] from them... ACTS 15:38

## 2. Leaders who disappoint you when they are under pressure

I have noticed that certain people avoid coming to church or participating when they are experiencing a domestic challenge or a financial problem. I am often under pressure from several quarters (looking after the Cathedral, dealing with situations concerning branches, pastors, lands and properties, personnel, salaries, letters, criticisms, telephone calls, emergencies, pressures of traveling and family). In the midst of all this, however, I must remain focused and perform all my duties.  It is important that I do not collapse or let people down when I am under pressure.

> *Confidence in an unfaithful man in time of trouble is like a*
> *broken tooth, and a foot out of joint.*     PROVERBS 25:19

There are some people who often present themselves with problems concerning homes and families. Have you noticed that these problems have not prevented them from going about their jobs? Any leader that deserts you when he is under pressure is a potentially dangerous person.

### Pastors Still Have to Preach

Pastors have to preach on Sunday mornings, sometimes even after having had a disagreement with their wives on the way to church. They still have to minister under the anointing. If they were to break down under pressure, they would be unreliable ministers.

### 3. Leaders who have moral weaknesses

If you have a leader with persistent episodes of immorality, take note of that person.  He or she could one day disappoint you or turn against you. Why?  Because the Bible says a leader must live a holy life, treating the young ladies as sisters and not as girlfriends.

> *[Treating] …the younger as sisters, with all purity.*
> 1 TIMOTHY 5:2

A person who lives continually in sin is often in rebellion against God. That attitude of rebellion can turn up in any of God's representatives at short notice.

### The Angry Pastor Walked out

You may also have to discipline such a fellow for his misdeeds. In his anger at your correction, he may walk out on you in rebellion. Such people usually go around, making up bad stories. You see, they have to give an explanation for leaving their church.

### 4. Leaders who have financial weaknesses

A thief is a person in rebellion against God. This rebellion will eventually turn against the pastors. If such a thief is confronted about his evil deeds, he is likely to become incensed against you. In his anger at being caught and corrected, he may also walk out and spread negative stories about you, claiming that you are the real thief! Remember that many traitors and rebels are also thieves.

> ...*he [Judas] was a thief...*   JOHN 12:6

### 5. Leaders who are worldly

A leader who loves watching pornography and highly sexualized films is to be noted. He loves worldly music and knows all the lyrics. Someone who admires worldliness is surely attracted to it. This person could desert you just as Demas deserted Paul.

> *For Demas hath forsaken me, having loved this present world...*
> 2 TIMOTHY 4:10

### 6. Leaders who think that they can do what you are doing better than you can

Anyone who is watching me as senior pastor might have these thoughts flashing through his mind: "I could do that better," or, "If given the chance, I would also be able to minister like that, and probably even be better." Such a person is dangerous to have around. Remember that Absalom thought he could do his father's job better than King David was doing it. Absalom said,

*...Oh that I were made judge in the land, that every man which hath any suit or cause might come unto me, and I would do him justice!* 2 SAMUEL 15:4

A person is not doing what he is doing because he is best at doing it. He is doing it because God has put him in that place. I am not the pastor of my church because I am the best pastor. I am here because God has placed me here. There may be pastors who are better pastors than I am, but God put me here instead of them.

David was the king because God made him king. He was not the king because he was the most qualified person. Sometimes an assistant may look even more capable at certain things than the head. But don't make the mistake of fighting against the order that God has set. You will not succeed! It is God who sets, and it is God who removes, as He so pleases. You cannot remove what God has set in place.

*And God hath set some in the church...* *1 Corinthians 12:28*

## 7. Any leader who will attack his own father or senior in ministry

Be careful of people who come to you from another church where they grew up. Mark them when they say all sorts of negative things about their former pastors and spiritual fathers in the Lord. Remember that Absalom was prepared to attack his own father.

*...Behold, my son [Absalom]... seeketh my life...*
2 SAMUEL 16:11

Such a person is deadly! Do not welcome such a person into your fold thinking that he will be loyal to you. Remember that he was thinking of attacking his own father. Absalom chased his own father out of town. Never befriend someone who attacks his own pastor.

I have listened as pastors said all sorts of negative things about their own seniors. Perhaps they thought they were gaining my sympathies, but the more they talked, the more "Absalomic" and treacherous I found them to be. This is why it is almost impossible to become a pastor in my church organization unless you grow into leadership from within.

### 8. Wounded leaders who have never recovered from their hurts

I observe closely all people who have been hurt by one event or the other. In normal church life, many things occur that can lead to hurts and offenses. I have discovered there are two types of people. One type recovers from the offense and moves ahead with his or her life. The other type seems to harbor lingering unforgiveness. Watch the latter of these people. They are potential defectors.

## Many Rebels Have Been Hurt Before

Almost every traitor has a history of being hurt at one time or the other. Just dig into the history of anarchists, and you will discover that they have been hurt by something that was said or done to them earlier. Remember how Absalom was furious at his brother Amnon for raping his sister Tamar.?

> ...*Absalom hated Amnon, because he had forced his sister Tamar.* 2 SAMUEL 13:22

Two years after this event, Absalom struck! The deep-seated wound finally produced fruit. All deep-seated wounds will one day bear the fruit of mutiny.

### 9. Leaders who are not prepared to be trained or retrained in the ministry

Take notice of a person who says things like, "I was a leader before I joined you," or "I have been a leader for many years in such-and-such church." What he is saying is, "I have already been trained, and your training program is unnecessary for me." Make no mistake, dear pastor and leader. People coming from other institutions need to be retrained to suit your needs. Do not allow anyone from another church to introduce another spirit or philosophy into the house.

## Are You an Old Tree?

Trees are either young or old. When a tree is young, it can be bent over; when it's old, it can no longer be bent. Do not try to bend an old tree. Or, using another analogy, do not try to teach an old dog new tricks.

**I have given up trying to retrain nice people from other churches.** Paul trained Timothy and told him exactly what to do. He told him what to preach and how to minister. He called him my son Timothy. Timothy was obviously prepared for training and retraining.

> *O Timothy, keep that which is committed to thy trust...*
> 1 TIMOTHY 6:20

## 10. Leaders who are not prepared to do menial jobs

Anyone who is not prepared to do menial jobs may be too lofty for real ministry. The disciples did menial jobs. They were ushers, waiters, errand boys and scavengers. **Without shame, they collected baskets of leftover breadcrumbs and fish bones in front of thousands of people.** They were sent on errands to buy food and to relay simple messages. I take very serious note of high and mighty individuals who think certain tasks are beneath them.

### The Lofty People

I have watched over the years as certain individuals within my flock refused to engage in menial jobs. They have rarely amounted to much in the ministry. I rebuke pastors and leaders who appear too stiff and too elitist to get involved in down-to-earth work. Jesus taught us the importance of being a hands-on leader.

> *...I am among you as he that serveth.* LUKE 22:27

That is why my Bible students are involved in scrubbing church toilets and cleaning floors. It helps them to become practical, more unpretentious leaders.

Watch out for "big shots." They won't amount to much in the ministry of the Lord Jesus Christ.

> *...Except ye... become as little children... ye shall not enter...*
> MATTHEW 18:3

### The Cafeteria Evangelist

Never forget Philip, the evangelist who was first sent to work in the church cafeteria. When he was asked to sort out all the problems of the church in relation to food, he did not say that it was beneath his dignity. He did not even mention that he was called to be an evangelist! In fact, it was because he was called to be an evangelist that God was giving him the opportunity to be dining hall prefect.

If God has called you to evangelize the world, you may have to start with menial jobs. Never forget that!

## 11. A leader with a persistently stormy marriage

Every marriage has difficulties. All honest people attest to that fact. But, take notice of people who have persistently unhappy homes. This is often because of pride and bad character. The person who is not able to keep his own home in order is not recommended to be a minister.

*One that ruleth well his own house...*   I TIMOTHY 3:4

In quarrelsome and unhappy marriages, you often have people that do not know how to apologize when they have done something wrong. If this characteristic spills over into the ministry, you will have turbulent and unhappy relationships between ministers and church members.

## 12. Leaders who are irritated and reactionary every time you correct them

A leader will often have to correct his subordinates. The person irritated by correction, surely must be questioned about his character. A true student will never become angry or overly irritated when you reprove him. He will welcome the redress that makes him a better person.

*Better is a poor and wise child than an old and foolish king,*
*who will no more be admonished.*   ECCLESIASTICS 4:13

The very fact that a person is irritated should tell you that he will not fit into your organization. Notice that Peter was neither irritated nor reactionary when Jesus rebuked him harshly.

*But he turned, and said unto Peter, Get thee behind me, Satan...* MATTHEW 16:23

### 13. A person who gives excuses and continually justifies himself

If a simple instruction turns into a prolonged debate, you are dealing with a possible anarchist. I remember one brother who misused some church equipment. When confronted, he denied it. A couple of weeks later, we came up with conclusive evidence that he had misused that equipment.

### He Continued Arguing

Would you believe that in spite of documented and irrefutable evidence, this leader argued his innocence for two more hours!? I just looked on in amazement. Remember to be careful of those who cannot admit their mistakes. Let us all learn from the example of King Saul, who justified himself when he had obviously disobeyed God. In spite of undeniable evidence, Saul insisted,

*...I have obeyed the voice of the LORD...* 1 SAMUEL 15:20

This stubborn denial is what made the Lord reject Saul and replace him with King David. Watch out for leaders who constantly deny any wrongdoing. It seems they are never wrong about anything. They never have anything to apologize about. They get angry and irritated when you seem to be unhappy about something they are doing. They turn the tables on you and make you feel that you are a hard taskmaster. The punishment for stubbornness is indeed severe -- rejection.

*...he hath also rejected thee from being king.* 1 SAMUEL 15:23

### 14. A person who does not keep promises

Watch out for brothers who make proposals to young ladies about marriage only to disappoint them a few months later. A person who regularly makes promises and breaks them is unreliable. Do not think that unfaithfulness will only be found in the arena of marital relationships. It will definitely spill over into his relationships with his colleagues, pastors and others.

> *...He that sweareth to his own hurt, and changeth not.*
> PSALM 15:4

Unfaithfulness is a character flaw that spreads through every sphere of a person's life. If he is unfaithful to his beloved (girlfriend), he is likely to be unfaithful to you one day. I respect people who say, "I will do this," and years later they do exactly what they said they would do.

### I Married Her

On the 26th of August 1985, I told my beloved (now, wife) that I would marry her one day. Five years later, I did! Watch people who keep their word on minor issues. They are likely to keep their word on major issues.

## 15. A leader who is vying for promotion and recognition

> *...Adonijah… exalted himself, saying, I will be king...*
> 1 KINGS 1:5

Adonijah was position-conscious. Although he was a prince, he wanted to be king himself. I once hinted to a leader that I intended to appoint him a pastor in the near future.

### The Pastor Could Not Wait

To my surprise, I found out that he had asked a little fellowship within the church to point to him and say, "Pastor, we love you." He could not wait for his public appointment. **Watch out for position-conscious people.** Many people have the position but do not do the job. Make sure your leaders are doing the job that goes with their position.

## 16. A person who is an unknown factor

Pastors, do not be naïve. Do not welcome little-known individuals into sensitive positions. Allow new people to stay around long enough before you make them leaders. An unknown factor is a dangerous factor.

Any new person is a potential traitor until proven otherwise. Remember that when the disciples had to choose someone to replace Judas, they picked one who had been with them long enough.

> *Wherefore of these men which have companied with us all the time... must one be ordained...* ACTS 1:21, 22

## 17. A leader who has never been criticized

A person who has never experienced criticism is often surprised when his superiors are under attack. He thinks there must be some truth in the criticism leveled against them. He usually thinks that if you do everything right, you will never be criticized! This is a great deception.

### Younger Ones Have Not Yet Been Criticized

This is a deception common to inexperienced leaders. An immature leader may even join the "enemy" if he feels they have a strong enough case.

I realize that no matter how hard you try to relate your experiences to certain people, they just cannot comprehend what you are saying.

A leader who has been through the fire of criticism is different from the leader who has never been criticized. When a mature person encounters slander and criticism in ministry, he handles it differently. He understands how the machinery of deception works. A mature person, like Christ, knows that these things are part of normal ministry.

> *...for it must needs be that offenses come...* MATTHEW 18:7

## 18. A leader who does not say "amen" or smile while you are preaching

Any loyal leader appreciates the sermons of his pastor. His support of and agreement with the pastor is demonstrated by his smile and may also be demonstrated by his vocalized "Amens." You cannot tell me that the expression on your face and your silence mean nothing. Silence means something. And the expression on your face means something.

### No Comment for Two Years!

The Bible says that Absalom said neither good nor bad for two years. How can you make no comment or remark for two whole years, and then after that invite me to a party? This is what Absalom did to his brother Amnon.

Absalom's silence and lack of response to his brother meant a lot. It meant murder was in the offing! Because God knows that a person's facial expression means something, he advised Ezekiel and Jeremiah not to be frightened by people's facial expressions.

*Be not afraid of their faces...* JEREMIAH 1:8

An unsmiling, grimacing leader who always has no comment to make must be watched.

## 19. A person who does not take notes when you are preaching

*...he said unto me, Write: for these words are true and faithful.*
REVELATION 21:5

The Bible teaches us to write down true and faithful words. Watch out for people who do not take notes while you are teaching. This could be a sign that they think that they know everything. A person who thinks he knows all that you are teaching should not be around you. He may be saying, "I'm as good as you. And there is nothing new that you can teach me!"

### He-Knows-it-All

During a community health lecture in the medical school, I learned a valuable lesson about handling public health education. We were taught that every time we ventured out to give a public lecture, we would need to psychologically overcome certain personalities in the audience. One of them was "the know-it-all." Know-it-alls do not take notes because they know it all. One thing you don't need is a know-it-all as an associate leader.

John the Apostle could not minister effectively to Diotrephes because he felt too big (preeminent) to receive from John. I believe this character in the Bible did not bother to take notes as John was preaching.

Diotrephes was too big to receive. John said that Diotrephes didn't receive him.

> ...but Diotrephes, who loveth to have the preeminence... receiveth us not.   3 JOHN 9

You might keep an eye on any leader that does not take notes when you preach.

### 20. A person who is not faithful in another person's work

Pay attention to people's attitudes toward their responsibilities. If they treat other people's businesses and properties with care, they are likely to treat your ministry with care. You never know how people behave when they are out of your sight. But when you see them, just observe how they handle someone else's car or property.

Watch out for the person who recklessly handles other people's belongings.

> And if ye have not been faithful in that which is another man's, who shall give you that which is your own?   LUKE 16:12

### 21. A leader who does not pay tithes and offerings

Anybody who goes to a restaurant with the intention of not paying for his meal is a dangerous character. Anyone who benefits from the church—but secretly does not support it—needs to be monitored.

#### Monitor Their Giving

I cannot monitor the tithes and offerings of the whole church. But I do monitor the tithes of my leaders. Any leader who does not pay his tithes could be a traitor. You see, money must not be a problem for any leader. The Bible teaches us that a person who does not give tithes is a robber.

> Will a man rob God? Yet ye have robbed me... In tithes and offerings.   MALACHI 3:8

I declare unto you therefore that every robber is a potential traitor. Watch him!

## 22. Leaders who do not attend certain meetings

Attending all relevant or required meetings is important for leaders. Take note of those who constantly regularly excuse themselves from certain meetings. They always have an excuse, but take note of them! Remember that Judas was always moving out on other missions when the disciples were fellowshipping with Christ. Remember how Thomas was absent when Christ appeared after His resurrection.

### Absentee Turns Traitor

I believe that it is because of Judas' frequent absenteeism that he became a traitor. I also think it is because Thomas missed a very important meeting that he became a doubter.

> But Thomas... was not with them when Jesus came.
> JOHN 20:24

The absence of certain leaders from some meetings most definitely will cause them to be different from your loyal team members.

Attendance at all important meetings is essential to maintaining loyalty. Do not overlook leaders who seem to be too busy to attend important discussions. After a while, such people will be different from the rest of your team.

## 23. A person who approves of someone making wrong decisions

> And he [Adonijah] conferred with Joab... and they... helped
> him.   1 KINGS 1:7

Joab approved of Adonijah's rebellious ideas. This was because Joab himself was a rebel. He had exhibited an independent spirit throughout the life and ministry of King David.

Notice the things that your leaders admire and become involved with. Observe the things that your team members approve of.

### What Do Your Leaders Admire?

Many years ago, a rebel in the making made favorable comments about another rebel. He spoke about how this dissident pastor seemed to be succeeding in his breakaway faction. He observed gleefully how this defector had acquired a new car shortly after rebelling. "He is having a good program!" he exclaimed. Only a few months later, this fellow staged his own rebellion.

## 24. Leaders who are not prepared to do things they did not choose to do

Leaders must be prepared to do what they are told to do. If you expect others to obey you, remember that it is first required of you to obey instructions. Some people want to sit where they want to sit and do what they want to do. Notice anyone who becomes reluctant in what he is doing because he is not doing what he prefers to do.

*Do all things without... disputings:* PHILIPPIANS 2:14

This Scripture is telling us to do all things joyfully – without arguments; even the things we don't feel like doing.

## 25. A person who poisons you about others

The cardinal thing everyone remembers about a snake (of the poisonous variety) is that it can poison you! Any Christian who poisons your mind about other people is a dangerous person. *Never forget that "He that speaks negatively about somebody to you will speak negatively about you to somebody."*

### The Slanderer in the Hotel

Mark the person who attempts to poison your mind about people you don't even know. I recall one time a famous evangelist came to Accra, the capital city of Ghana. My friend happened to be the manager of the hotel that this evangelist visited. Because he was in and out of the hotel room, my manager friend overheard a local pastor lambasting another minister of the city.

### He Poisoned the Evangelist

As he listened, my friend told me that the famous evangelist's mind was thoroughly poisoned about this other minister. Before this minister had the opportunity to introduce himself, the slanderer had gone to work. The word slanderer in the New Testament is translated from the Greek word diabolos, which means "devil."

*...not slanderers, sober, faithful in all things.* 1 TIMOTHY 3:11

Learn here and now that a person who spews out negative things about others is a devil. I didn't say so, the Bible says so. Slanderer means devil. A slanderer is a devil.

## 26. A leader who is not prepared to be birthed into the philosophy, the standards, the vision, the procedures and the spirit of the house

Every church is different. We all believe that Jesus Christ is the Son of God. However, the philosophy, the standards, the vision and the procedures of each church can be very different. This is what the Bible calls the due order of a ministry -- the way things are done there.

### Every Church Has a Due Order

*...for that we sought him not after the due order.*
1 CHRONICLES 15:13

Any new person must be prepared to acclimatize and adapt himself to the new environment. A person who often says, "In my old church, we did things like that..." and, "I think that a better way to do this is how I used to do it in my former church," is a person who should be watched. He probably hasn't fully adapted to the spirit of the house. That is why he is constantly making references to his previous place of ministry. The Israelites never adapted to their new circumstances in Babylon. They were never birthed into the spirit of their new homes. And this was evident in their songs,

*...we wept, when we remembered Zion.* PSALM 137:1

## 27. A person who manipulates his way into leadership without serving his way into that leadership position

Every Christian leader is supposed to serve his way into a leadership position. Joshua was a servant of Moses. Elisha was the servant of Elijah. Elisha became the next major prophet by serving Elijah for many years. In fact, once when the king was looking for a prophet, they immediately thought of finding someone who had served Elijah.

> But Jehosophat said, Is there not here a prophet... [They] answered... Here is Elisha... which poured water on the hands of Elijah.    2 KINGS 3:11

Certain people pose as mature and already seasoned leaders who don't need to serve. They exert certain airs and manipulate inexperienced leaders. They sometimes have certain skills that the church desperately needs. The pastor may unknowingly appoint such a person to a leadership position. He may then realize that this fellow has not served his way through the normal ranks. Such a person can be dangerous, because one day he may try to manipulate his way into other positions. He may even try to replace you!

## 28. A leader who does not stay around to mingle and interact with other church members

If you are a leader of God's people, surely you will want to interact with them and get to know them. Are you just occupying a high-sounding position, or are you a true shepherd? Remember that the hireling doesn't care about the sheep, but the true shepherd cares and wants to be near them.

### Prime Minister or Pastor?

I always stay around after ministering to interact with the congregation. I do this even though I am often tired and exhausted. A true leader does this because he is genuinely interested in the flock. I don't believe in being whisked away by a chauffeur-driven car.

Some pastors behave more like an aloof Prime Minister than a shepherd of God's flock. Are you a Prime Minister or a shepherd?

*I am the good shepherd, and know my sheep, and am known of mine.*  JOHN 10:14

## 29. A leader who has a "Jezebel" for a wife

Jezebel was a wife who pushed her husband into doing wrong things. **Every experienced pastor must not only look at a leader's character but also at the leader's wife.** A wife has a great influence on her husband. She can either make or break him. A "Jezebellic" wife may encourage her husband to have things which don't really belong to him. Just because Ahab was the king did not mean that he owned all land in the nation. But Jezebel encouraged her husband to take over Naboth's vineyard even though it did not belong to him.

### Watch the Position-Conscious Wife

If your associate has a Jezebel for a wife, she will push him into improper things without him even realizing it. He could find himself stretching out his hand to take what does not belong to him. Many pastors' wives are responsible for making their husbands discontent.

They suggest to their husbands:

"By now we should have such and such a car."

"Is the senior pastor the only one who must travel to conferences?"

"By now, you should have your own church."

Jezebel planted evil thoughts in her husband's mind.

*And Jezebel his wife said unto him, Dost thou now govern the kingdom... arise and eat bread...*  1 KINGS 21:7

These "Jezebellic" inspirations will spur a good pastor on into things that he never really intended to do. **So do not only consider the leader; but also observe his wife carefully.** Remember the adage: husband may be the head, but the wife is the neck.

## 30. A person who constantly shifts the blame to other people

A good leader does not shift blame. As a leader, you bear ultimate responsible for everything that happens.

### Bad Leaders Quickly Say, "It's Your Fault!"

I do not know why some leaders never want to take any blame. We are all to blame sometimes. A strong and true leader shoulders the blame for everything. Something bad had happened in our church. At a meeting of the pastors, I told them it was my fault. They were surprised because they didn't know how that unfortunate event even related to me.

But I pointed out to them that I was to blame because I was the overall head leader. When two bad leaders meet, they will accuse each other of being at fault.

### Good Leaders Say, "It's My Fault!"

When two good leaders meet, they fight to take the responsibility for any mishap. Remember how Adam shifted the blame to his wife? And how the wife shifted the blame to the serpent? Unfortunately, the serpent had no one to shift the blame to.

> *...The woman whom thou gavest to be with me, she gave me...*
> GENESIS 3:12

### 31. A leader who thinks too much money is being spent on the Head

Remember how Judas opposed the expensive gift given to his pastor, Jesus? Most people who really love their pastors feel that nothing is too good for him. A trait of disloyalty may manifest itself when other loyal people begin to appreciate the pastor. Out of guilty feelings that the disloyal leader may have, he does not get involved when there is a show of appreciation for the pastor. Remember the words of the traitor Judas,

> *Why was not this ointment sold for three hundred pence, and given to the poor?* JOHN 12:5

Like all disloyal people, Judas felt it was a waste to spend such an amount of money on the pastor.

### 32. A leader who is unduly quiet, reserved and detached

Take note of people who always have no comment to make and nothing to contribute. The Bible says that Absalom said nothing for two years. After being quiet for two years, he decided to have a party. The quietness and moodiness of Absalom had a meaning.

### The Quietness Can Mean Something

Unfortunately, Amnon and King David did not detect anything wrong with Absalom's reserved demeanor. However, it did mean that something evil was in the making. Watch out for those who are unusually calm and detached, especially when you know that they normally make positive contributions and comments.

### 33. A leader who is always late for meetings

Chronic lateness to important meetings can be evidence of a wrong attitude. Perhaps an attitude of "I know what they are going to say at the meeting." or "I will come when it is necessary." Such a person might be nursing a scornful and arrogant spirit. Pride always leads to conflicts within organizations.

> *Cast out the scorner, and contention shall go out...*
> PROVERBS 22:10

Lateness can reflect the unwillingness of the person to be a part of the meeting. He may wish he did not have to be around. Therefore he cannot bear to be at the meeting for a complete session. Before you receive a resignation letter from your assistant, you may find him often arriving late to meetings.

### 34. A leader who feels he knows the mindset of the organization and therefore does not bother to ask important questions

I recall a leader being questioned as to why he did not bother to find out about an important issue.

### I Knew What You Would Say

"I knew what you would say, so I didn't bother to ask," he answered. "I know how you analyze such cases anyway."

In reality, this person was saying that, "I'm dealing with unreasonable personalities who will never understand me anyway. There was no point in my coming to see you." A person who views you as being unreasonable is obviously not loyal to you in his heart.

### 35. A leader who has not been involved in practical ministry work

I don't understand how someone can teach at a Bible school unless he has been involved in the work of the ministry himself. The ministry of the Lord Jesus is not a set of theories. It is practical down-to-earth hard work. A person who has not been involved in the basics of ministry work is still a theoretician. All he has to offer are theories about what is right and wrong.

> *Not a novice...*   1 TIMOTHY 3:6

Such a person could turn against you because of his theoretical inclinations. No wonder good Bible schools only accept seasoned ministers as instructors. We need people who have seen the practical workings of the Lord Jesus, the Holy Spirit and the Word of God. People who have lived through successes, mistakes, betrayals, and the highs and the lows of ministry have much more to offer as a teacher.

Isn't it amazing how it's always the ones who are doing nothing for God who know how things should be done!

### 36. A leader who does not contribute to a joint effort which is intended to bless and appreciate their pastor

Take notice of those associates who do not get involved in projects intended to honor their superiors. If the non-involvement isn't for lack of money, it is usually out of disloyalty.

### 37. A leader who has not been tested by time

Dear Christian friend, in this very last sign I am pointing out a very important reality. Time reveals many important things. The Bible says,

> *For many are called, but few are chosen.*   MATTHEW 22:14

Time reveals the differences between those chosen and those called. Time alone will separate the men from the boys. Many of our theories and analyses are only proven by time. **If you want to know if someone will be loyal, commend the person to God and to time.**

# Signs of Disloyalty

*(For reasons of privacy you may want to make notes on a photocopy of this page.)*

## Chapter Five- My Action Plan:

In reflecting on the 37 signs of disloyalty discussed, list the top three to five that most caught your attention:

(1) No. _____ _____

    1. Who should I discuss this with?

    2. What further thought, plan or action is needed?

(2) No. _____ _____

    1. Who should I discuss this with?

    2. What further thought, plan or action is needed?

(3) No. _____ _____

    1. Who should I discuss this with?

    2. What further thought, plan or action is needed?

(4) No. _____ _____

    1. Who should I discuss this with?

    2. What further thought, plan or action is needed?

(5) No. _____    _____

　　1. Who should I discuss this with?


　　2. What further thought, plan or action is needed?

CHAPTER 6

# From the Lips of Treacherous Men

*...out of the abundance of the heart the mouth speaketh.*
MATTHEW 12:34

Many disloyal people are given away by their words spoken, especially in an unguarded moment. The Bible also tells us,

*...the tree is known by his fruit.* MATTHEW 12:33

The next time you stand next to a tree wondering what species it is, just look for evidence of its fruit. The fruit of the tree reveals its species.

What follows here are some interesting quotations that I have collected over the years. These sayings, from the lips of disloyal people, strike me whenever I hear them.

I can remember the day I heard each of these statements. Some were said to me personally, although many are things I heard about. These statements tell you a lot about the personalities involved and about the condition of their hearts.

Let's begin with this statement the right-hand man of a pastor of a very large church.

### 1. "Some of us could be head pastors. It is just that we have decided to submit."

This statement comes from an associate, who, after analyzing his head pastor for a while, has begun to see himself as just as capable as his head. He probably thinks he is in the second or third position mistakenly or by an unfortunate play of circumstances. Such thoughts can arise when assistants or associates are allowed to step into the shoes of their head for a brief season.

This often happens when the head pastor may have been away for a period. They were given the opportunity to preach once or twice, and some people said that they were blessed. This associate begins to think that he is as good as or even better than his head.

### 2. "I would like you to pray with me about certain things that are going on at the office – the way I am being treated."

This gentleman thought he was being mistreated by the administration of his church. He went around discussing this with ordinary church members. He solicited their prayers, but in reality he was spreading dissent and mistrust.

It was a subtle way of getting other people involved in his feelings of discontent. He was indirectly gaining the sympathy and support for what he considered to be mistreatment. This is the political stage of disloyalty. By the time this pastor had finished spreading his story, the church was full of confused members who saw the senior pastors as unreasonable.

Eventually, this pastor defected and left behind a miserable, divided and untrusting group. It took over a year for this church to recover from the lies that had been spread. It took almost two years to restore a healthy environment.

### 3. "He (the senior pastor) has deviated from the original vision and course."

I heard the associate of one mega-church declare that his pastor had deviated from the principal course of the Bible.

### He Doesn't Read the Bible Anymore

He claimed that his pastor didn't read the Bible anymore and studied secular books on leadership instead.

But this was a misrepresentation of the truth. This statement, although it sounded like a valid accusation, was actually a manifestation of disloyalty. The associate was simply not prepared to flow anymore with new ideas that the visionary would come up with. He had assisted for years, but now a disloyal spirit made him criticize every move of his pastor.

### 4. "I will not come. I will not go. I will not be transferred."

Remember that during the rebellion of Korah, Dathan and Abiram refused to go when Moses called for them.

> *And Moses sent to call Dathan and Abiram, the sons of Eliab:*
> *which said, We will not come up:*  NUMBERS 16:12

When a person is "too big" to be sent, then he probably is too big for the organization. He or she is now too much of a big shot to be "pushed" around. When a leader declares that he will not move, decide to move him away from you permanently.

### 5. "Would you do that yourself?"

In an army, when the Colonel or General asks the troops to move out to attack, no member of the platoon dares ask the Colonel or the General if he would go on such a mission himself. None would dare to ask, "Would you risk your life to do what you are sending us to do?" Although it is a legitimate question, it reeks of insubordination and defiance. Such words only come from the heart of a rebel.

### 6. "Many people are saying...Even the workers and elders are saying that..."

This statement, as we discussed in the political stage of disloyalty, implies that you have been talking to people about your leader in a negative way. People realize your disloyalty and the disapproval that you have for your superior. This is why they are able to say negative things to you about him.

A disloyal person has his or her ear tuned to hear the negative things people are saying. Take note of anyone who comes up to you with such phrases as "many people are saying..., a lot of people are saying...," etc.

### 7. "You are not always right."

I remember the day a subordinate pastor told me that I was not always right. At the time, I brushed aside the statement. But as I thought over it, I realized that nobody is ever always right. No one, apart from God, is ever 100 percent correct.

This "insurrectionist" was actually giving me another message. He was saying, "You are having your way as usual. But this time, you are not right." He was telling me that he did not support me in what I was doing. He was informing me that he would just flow along because I had the veto power. His eyes blazed with hatred as he said the words, *"You are not always right."*

### 8. "You are proud and difficult to work with. You are stubborn."

This person no longer admires or trusts his leader's decisions. These are the words of a person who is critical and untrusting. A good leader has to be firm and strong. **When a person is consumed with disloyalty, he sees strength and firmness as stubbornness and pride.** If you look at your leader through the eyes of love, you will see how great a person he is. However, if you look at him through the eyes of rebellion, you will see evil in him.

### 9. "A pastor colleague of mine was told, 'Pastor, there is a lot of fear in this church. But I want you to know that I don't fear you.'"

This person has a spirit of defiance. What he's actually saying is, "I will fight you if necessary because I don't fear you."

### 10. A pastor friend of mine was told by his church member after a service, " You remind me of my father. He is so full of himself."

This person was telling her pastor that his confidence reeked of pride and arrogance. When a church member tells a pastor, "You are arrogant and proud," she is not admiring him, but rather demeaning him. Her heart is not full of commitment, but filled with disloyalty. "Pastor, you are full of yourself."

**11. An associate pastor said about his head pastor, "When he's away, the church grows, and many more people attend the services."**

In other words, this associate pastor was saying in other words that the presence of the head pastor is undesirable; that people in the congregation dislike the contribution of the head pastor. No loyal pastor would ever speak about his head in such a way.

**12. I once asked an associate pastor, "How is your senior pastor doing?"**

He replied, "I don't know where he is."

Then I asked, "How come? Don't you see him regularly?"

He answered, **"Not at all. This yessa master, yessa master, yessa master cannot go on forever."**

By saying these words, this associate pastor was ridiculing the beautiful and orderly relationship that exists between the head leader and his subordinate. He was depicting it as a demeaning slave-master relationship. I don't even need to tell you that a short while later, this associate turned out to be an ungrateful separatist.

**13. "I don't see why everybody is making such a fuss about that breakaway pastor!"**

In this statement, the pastor was indirectly approving of rebellion and church splits. No wonder that in due time, he became a rebel.

**14. I asked a pastor, "How was the visit of your senior to the town? Was it successful?" He replied, "Oh yes, it was fine. We had a good time. But you know our man, he likes expensive Chinese restaurants."**

Here again, a pastor is making a sarcastic and critical remark about his senior leader. It may seem like a passing remark, but it reeks of contempt.

**15. A disloyal assistant pastor once said to his leader, "You don't have any idea what people are saying about you. You don't know what I've had to tell them."**

This disloyal pastor is letting you know that your support within the church is waning. He is informing you that he has had to stabilize feelings of discontent in the congregation. He is informing you that you are unpopular and not as great as you may think.

### 16. "I admire your style of leadership. In our church, our man (the head pastor) doesn't give us many opportunities."

This pastor is expressing his dissatisfaction with his home church. By saying it so openly, he is showing that he is not loyal or protective of his own church. He is now openly exposing its deficiencies and shortcomings.

# From the Lips of Treacherous Men

*(For reasons of privacy you may want to make notes on a photocopy of this page.)*

## Chapter Six- My Action Plan:

1. When have I had disloyal words spoken to me?

    a. The situation?

    b. By whom?

    c. Did I recognize the disloyalty at the time?

    d. What was the outcome?

2. When have I spoken disloyal words? (Be brutally honest.)

    a. The situation?

    b. To whom?

    c. Did I realize what I was doing at the time?

    d. What was the outcome?

    e. Is there forgiveness I need to seek?

# CHAPTER 7

# A Loyal Assistant

An assisting minister is anyone operating in a position such as associate pastor, assistant or deputy pastor, worship leader, departmental pastor, youth pastor, branch pastor, minister of music, etc. The duties of an assisting minister may appear obvious. It may even seem superfluous to write about what is expected in that role. But I have found the assisting minister to be one of the most important people on a ministry team. He or she can make or break the ministry by his or her actions, words and even attitude. From experience I have learned that it is better to have no assistant, than to have a bad assistant. It is better to have no branch church than to have a branch church with a bad branch pastor.

## A Good Ambassador

A good assistant minister can be compared to a good ambassador. He does not reflect his own ideas and visions, but rather those of his home country (senior minister). In some ways, a good assistant minister can be compared to the biblical role of a good wife. **He must not only obey instructions, but also genuinely support and flow with the head or**

**senior pastor.** He must not be an independent and uncooperative person.

If you are not faithful in another man's ministry, do not ever expect to have anything of your own.

> *And if ye have not been faithful in that which is another man's, who shall give you that which is your own?* LUKE 16:12

There is a proliferation of associate Absaloms, Adonijahs, Ahithophels, Shemeis, Joabs, Judases and Lucifers in the church. These are the major rebels of the Bible. Any experienced minister will have had his fair share of these personalities. I am against these people, and I am teaching against these personalities. Decide that you will never become a rebel.

### It Is Not Easy to Be the Head Leader

It is not easy to be the head of anything. All of the responsibility falls on you. You are always to blame for what goes wrong because you are the ultimate head. In a certain sense, it is easier to be an assistant than it is to be a head person. But in another sense it is difficult to always submit, follow and support.

### You Must Be Called to Assist

I believe it is a gift and a calling to be a good associate. If God has not called you to stand in the place of an assisting leader, do not take it upon yourself to perform this frustrating and difficult task. Decide to be your own person from the beginning. If you are the head, you must ensure that you have loyal associates. Anyone who is actually called to be a head leader, but acts as an assistant, will be a bad assistant.

Here are some lessons that will help you function effectively in the role of an assistant. **If you are going to assist, then do it well!** I believe these are perceptive, discerning and important instructions.

## TWENTY-NINE WAYS TO BE A GOOD ASSISTANT
**1. Make mention of your senior pastor often, and in a favorable light.**

Do this whenever you are speaking, preaching or counseling.

## 2. Quote your leader as often as possible.

As I said earlier, you are actually an ambassador representing him. Jesus is supposed to be the most important person in the church and not the pastor. He must be magnified and not anyone else. He said,

> ...if I be lifted up from the earth, will draw all men unto me.
> JOHN 12:32

However, there is a certain respect and admiration you must have for the head pastor. Do not use your pastor as the illustration of a bad example. Rather, always speak of your head as someone to be admired and followed. In every institution, a particular person must be more prominent, and that is the head leader.

### Anything with Two Heads Is a Beast

If more than one person is prominent, you have a situation where there are two heads -- a freak. Regularly mention the fact that what you are doing is on behalf of the head pastor. This makes it clear that there are not two heads, but just one.

## 3. Genuinely admire your pastor and praise him often.

If you do not admire your leader, you should not be working with him in the first place! If you are a good assistant, you will see the wisdom decisions your head makes. You will admire the way he preaches and the revelations he brings forth. A bad assistant is full of contempt for all that his head does.

I learned some time ago that you receive teaching best from people you admire. This is a secret to catching the anointing. If you admire other leaders, but have no admiration for your own, I submit that you are in the wrong place.

## 4. Introduce your pastor in an exciting way and make positive or complimentary remarks about what he has preached.

Make statements like, "I was really blessed today by this message," or "That message was timely." A loyal associate is full of genuine public compliments for his pastor's sermon. When the associate makes these open remarks, the whole church appreciates their pastor's message even more!

### 5. Announce the visit or arrival of your pastor with excitement.

We are all excited to see someone we love. A good associate will announce the arrival of his head pastor with joy and introduce him with pride. Surely the fact that you are not happy to see him would mean that something is wrong.

### Don't Allow Him In!

I remember a church that had a rebellious pastor. When the general overseer came to visit, the pastor instructed the ushers not to allow him to enter the building. Can you believe that? The overall head was physically prevented from entering a church he had founded. A rebellious person is not happy to see his pastor. But a loyal person welcomes his spiritual father with joy.

### 6. Do not become a receiver of complaints.

Let people know that if they want to grumble and criticize, they have come to the wrong person. If your office is a center for the discussion of the shortcomings of your pastor, then surely you are another Absalom in the making! It takes a certain evil spirit for people to have enough confidence to bring to you all their accusations. Unity begins with the most senior associate. If he is loyal, the others will follow.

### 7. You must find genuine excuses for any lapses of your head pastor.

Everybody makes mistakes, and nobody is always right. Your senior will have his fair share of mistakes. **It is your duty as a good assistant to defend and protect the developing ministry of your pastor.**

For example, if the head is late for an important function, a good assistant will offer a suitable explanation for this lapse. Emphasize that something must have happened to hold him up.

### He Is Always Late

Off-hand remarks like "He's always late anyway," or "He's probably sleeping as usual," put your pastor in a bad light. They are a sign of disloyalty!

**8. Whenever your senior pastor is unable to attend a function, you must inform the parties concerned that he had intended to be there himself but could not make it for very important reasons.**

Give the impression that your head is a good person who was constrained by real and pressing issues. Do not say, "Oh, I do not know why he didn't come to the hospital to visit you. He was sleeping at home when I last called."

**9. Always remind the congregation that you are not the main pastor.**

When people praise you and are impressed with your ministry, appreciate their words, but happily remind them that there is someone above you. Notice what John the Baptist did when people were so pleased with his ministry.

He said,

> *...I am not the Christ but... I am sent...*   JOHN 3:28

If you are not willing to let others know that there is someone more senior to you, then surely your loyalty is deficient.

**10. The good assistant tells his admiring congregation where he learned all that he knows.**

Jesus often said,

> *...The Son can do nothing of himself, but what he seeth the Father do...*   JOHN 5:19

**11. When you minister to church members, let them know that you are doing this on behalf of the head pastor and not on your own behalf.**

When we say "In the name of Jesus," it signals to people that we are acting on behalf of Jesus, our Head. For instance, all ministers on earth represent Christ. We do not come in our own name. We come in the name of Jesus.

### 12. Be genuinely happy at the promotion of your pastor.

Do not secretly think that he does not deserve the fame and popularity he may be getting. Notice what John the Baptist said when the popularity of Jesus was reported to him: "Behold... all men come to him." Notice again the classic reply of a good assistant:

> *He must increase, but I must decrease.*   JOHN 3:30

A bad associate gets worried when his pastor is promoted. He feels he is being left behind and people will see too great a difference between the lead pastor and himself.

### 13.  Ensure that everything is well with your senior pastor.

Ensure that he is properly seated and is comfortable. Give up your own chair if necessary. Be sure that he is acknowledged and respected by everyone. This is the joyful duty of a good assistant.

### 14. Be genuinely excited at the arrival and involvement of your head pastor in any function.

Announce the visit of your pastor to your department or branch with excitement. If you see his visit or involvement as an intrusion or a bother, then the problem is with you. You may be a rebellious and independent assistant at heart.

### 15.  Honor your pastor's wife as well.  Minister to her.

I take note of any person who doesn't respect my wife. It is an important sign to me. If you receive my wife, you have received me. In the same way, if you disrespect and disregard my wife, you have done the same to me.

> *He that receiveth you receiveth me...*   MATTHEW 10:40

### 16.  Regard your association with your head pastor as a learning experience.

Decide to learn something from him everyday. A good assistant or deputy or associate learns from his head leader; the bad associate sees many mistakes in him.

### Two Pastors, Two Opinions

I remember the time two pastors visited from their branch churches outside Accra, Ghana. They were present on a Sunday morning as I ministered. Later, we had a meeting with all of the visiting pastors.

One told me, "As I listened to you minister on Sunday morning, I thought to myself, 'This man is repeating himself.' He went over these points in last week's sermon," "However," he continued, "I happened to speak to the other visiting branch pastor who thought otherwise."

This other branch pastor also commented on the Sunday service. He said, "I really enjoyed Sunday's message. The Bishop was very relaxed as he emphasized the points from the previous week's sermon. It helped the congregation understand the message even better."

### Repetition or Good Teaching?

While one pastor saw the repetition as useless -- even harmful-- the other saw it as an effective teaching approach. These two pastors confirmed what I have believed all along. You can either view your relationship with your head pastor as a learning experience or as a fault-finding mission. A good assistant is always learning something new. A bad assistant is always tired and bored.

### 17. Acquire your pastor's tapes.

Soak in his messages on audio and video tapes. Catch the anointing on his life through faithfulness and loyalty.

### 18. In your preaching, do not hesitate to refer to your pastor as an example of a successful person.

Use your pastor as an illustration of noble things.

### 19. Flow with decisions and policies made by your head pastor. Do this even if you have a different opinion.

Only one idea can work at a time. Only one strategy can be implemented at a time. If you are the associate, submit to the leader. You may say, "I don't think this is the right thing to do, but if that is the decision you have taken. I will abide by it."

**20. A good assistant does not establish a private, side-fellowship in the church without the knowledge or approval of his pastor.**

**21. Periodically organize pleasant surprises for your pastor.**

Spontaneously celebrate the birthday of your pastor and bring gifts. This will help draw you closer to his heart. The church will be full of the love of God.

**22. When your head is going on a journey, be at the airport or the station to see him off. It is also important to be there to welcome him back with joy.**

On appropriate occasions organize a 'Welcome Home' party. Show that you are glad to have the pastor back home. A bad assistant will say, "If he is going, let him go. He has a wife, I'm sure she will see him off."

**23. During counseling sessions, learn to assist properly.**

First of all, the assisting minister must not contribute counsel that is contrary to what is being said. He must also not try to develop a different train of thought, which may confuse the one receiving counsel. Do not try to impress with some "high-sounding" wisdom.

### Just Emphasize What Your Pastor Says

Simply help your senior say better what he is saying and emphasize what he has already said. Do not remain quiet during counseling sessions, as this will only make you look like a spectator and make the counselee feel awkward.

I teach all assisting ministers to use these simple but very powerful phrases when assisting their seniors in counseling. These phrases can be introduced at intervals during the counseling session.

1. Do you understand what the pastor is saying?
2. Do you understand that the pastor is only trying to help you?
3. The pastor is only saying this because he loves you.

4. I wish I had had someone speak to me in this way when I was in a similar situation.

By offering comments like these as the senior minister counsels, you lend greater impact to his words.

## 24. A loyal assistant takes notes at meetings while his senior pastor is talking or ministering.

Realize that it takes a certain amount of humility to take notes when someone is talking. That is why not writing notes is significant. Taking notes means that you are learning something.

### Writing Notes Expresses Humility

Note-taking means that someone senior with more insight than you is imparting knowledge to you. If the most senior associate writes notes, it will encourage others to do as well. All my pastors, from the most senior to the least of them, take notes when I am speaking.

## 25. A loyal assistant personally gives gifts to his senior pastor or ministry leader.

### Why a Gift?

*A man's gift maketh room for him, and bringeth him before great men.* PROVERBS 18:16

A gift means a thousand different things. It means the giver loves you, he appreciates you, he respects you and he honors you. It also means the associate admires you; thinks well of you and wants to be like you.

A gift also sends a message of encouragement, telling the senior pastor or leader that he or she has been a real blessing. A gift also says, "I want the anointing that is upon you." These are the opposite of evil thoughts, and they displace (to some extent) traitorous plans.

The senior pastor or ministry leader may not necessarily need the gift. But the giver's act of giving it is needed! When a person ministers to you with a gift, a thousand messages are spoken.

**26. A loyal assistant is protective of his Senior Pastor. He is prepared to defend against any problems arising out of his pastor's mistakes.**

Everyone is capable of making mistakes. I can assure you that every senior pastor will make many mistakes, large and small, during his ministry. Woe to you, if you have a disloyal assistant by your side, when you make a blunder. A loyal assistant will seek to cushion the negative effect of your mistake and protect you.

**27. A good assistant is not ignorant of the fact that his pastor is human and capable of making mistakes.**

A good assistant constantly prays for his pastor or ministry leader. He hopes for the best and prays that God will keep them all on the right track. He sees himself as someone who is linked to his senior pastor or leader. They sink or swim together. A good associate does not think of his leader as being infallible. He knows that any pastor or leader can and does make some mistakes. This is why he prays so hard for him or her.

**28. A good assistant gives his head pastor wise counsel. He does not feed him with false praises or flatteries.**

A good assistant knows that he is very close to his leader or head pastor. He knows that his input may be the most valuable. He knows the damaging effects of flattering his senior pastor or leader and misleading him.

**29. A good associate is content to be an assistant.**

A good associate is happy in his position. Pastors and leaders must look out for the spirit of contentment in assisting workers. A content assistant does not covet his leader's or pastor's position or any personal possessions.

> *Thou shall not covet... any thing that is thy neighbor's.*
> EXODUS 20:17

# The Loyal Assistant

*(For reasons of privacy you may want to make notes on a photocopy of this page.)*

## Chapter Seven- My Action Plan:

- **I AM an assistant.** Checkmark below the practices I already follow or need to follow.
- **I HAVE an assistant.** Circle the check box below for the practices he or she already follows or needs to follow.
- Schedule a helpful discussion with your assistant or leader about your thoughts.

1. ☐ Make mention of your senior pastor often and in a favorable light.
2. ☐ Quote your leader as often as possible.
3. ☐ Genuinely admire your pastor and praise him often.
4. ☐ Introduce your pastor in an exciting way and make positive or complimentary remarks about what he has preached.
5. ☐ Announce the visit or arrival of your pastor with excitement.
6. ☐ Do not become a receiver of complaints.
7. ☐ You must find genuine excuses for any lapses of your head pastor.
8. ☐ Whenever your senior pastor is unable to attend a function, you must inform the parties concerned that he had intended to be there himself but could not make it for very important reasons.
9. ☐ Always remind the congregation that you are not the main pastor.
10. ☐ The good assistant tells his admiring congregation where he learned all that he knows.
11. ☐ When you minister to church members, let them know that you are doing this on behalf of the head pastor and not on your own behalf.
12. ☐ Be genuinely happy at the promotion of your pastor.
13. ☐ Ensure that everything is well with your senior pastor.
14. ☐ Be genuinely excited at the arrival and involvement of your head pastor in any function.

15. ☐ Honor your pastor's wife as well. Minister to her.

16. ☐ Regard your association with your head pastor as a learning experience.

17. ☐ Acquire your pastor's tapes or recordings.

18. ☐ In your preaching, do not hesitate to refer to your pastor as an example of a successful person.

19. ☐ Flow with decisions and policies made by your head pastor. Do this even if you have a different opinion.

20. ☐ A good assistant does not establish a private, side-fellowship in the church without the knowledge or approval of his pastor.

21. ☐ Periodically organize pleasant surprises for your pastor.

22. ☐ When your head pastor is going on a journey, be at the airport or station to see him off. It is also important to be there to welcome him back with joy.

23. ☐ During counseling sessions, learn to assist properly.

24. ☐ A loyal assistant takes notes at meetings while his senior pastor is talking or ministering.

25. ☐ A loyal assistant personally gives gifts to his senior pastor or ministry leader.

26. ☐ A loyal assistant is protective of his Senior Pastor. He is prepared to defend against any problems arising out of his pastor's mistakes.

27. ☐ A good assistant is not ignorant of the fact that his pastor is human and capable of making mistakes.

28. ☐ A good assistant gives his head pastor wise counsel. He does not feed him with false praises or flatteries.

29. ☐ A good associate is content to be an assistant.

CHAPTER 8

# A Disloyal Assistant

A bad assistant is often difficult to detect, but the Bible teaches us to mark those that cause divisions. Senior ministers and senior leaders can use the following signs to identify disloyal behavior in assistants or associate ministers. And honest branch churches, assistant ministers and other leaders who identify with any of these traits can also use them to evaluate disloyal tendencies in themselves. Senior church leaders take note, when an assistant exhibits any of the following characteristics.

## TWENTY CHARACTERISTICS OF DISLOYAL ASSISTANTS

**1. When things go wrong, unfaithful assistants are quick to say, "I knew all along that this would not work."**

This quickly surfaces because they were not in full support of the idea from the very beginning. Therefore, they feel vindicated when something they opposed goes wrong. Any assistant who is happy that things have gone poorly is disloyal and must be displaced and replaced.

**2. When you come up with a suggestion, new idea or vision, they have**

**no comment to make – either good or bad.**

Silence, especially in times of trouble, often indicates your assistant is not in full agreement.

### 3. A disloyal assistant often thinks, "I would be a better leader than my superior if I just had the chance!"

He is often thinking that he should actually be in the top spot. A good assistant does not think that way. He is conscious of how difficult it must be to be the leader in charge. He has no wish to replace his superior but is content to continue assisting until the very end.

### 4. A dissatisfied assistant is not happy about the differences between himself and his superior that make him look subordinate.

A bad assistant wants to have all that his boss or senior leader has. He wants to have the same authority, the same status, a similar income and the same car. He sees no reason why there should be a difference. He does not like it when people see a difference between himself and his head pastor.

### 5. He is very concerned about his image rather than being concerned about raising the image of the one he assists.

John the Baptist was a good associate of Christ. He said Jesus must become more important and more prominent than he was.

*He must increase, but I must decrease.* JOHN 3:30

That is the attitude of a good assistant. A bad assistant gets irritated at the slightest event that in any way lowers his image. He will ask you, "Why did you talk to me that way when we were outside?" If you instruct him in public, he will pretend that he is not even listening. He gives the impression to the flock that although he is an associate, he is his own boss.

### 6. A treacherous assistant will eagerly look for opportunities to walk in his leader's shoes.

Such bad assistants cannot wait for opportunities to preach in place of their superior. They eagerly look forward to the time when he or she travels so they can pose as the leader. This can get so bad that when the leader is away, the disloyal assistant will actually use their leader's office and make decisions they are not entitled to make. In contrast, a good assistant constantly realizes that he is not the senior leader and cannot fit into his position.

**7. The bad assistant sees all the faults and mistakes in the senior minister's life. He rarely sees the good things.**

The disloyal assistant sees mostly the mistakes in what his or her leader says or does. He thinks the senior leader does not speak well in public. He thinks the senior pastor prolongs the services. He takes note of the ways people are offended by how the head leader has spoken to them. In other words, the bad assistant catalogues the "sins" of his leader. *But he has no such catalogue of his leader's good attributes.*

**8. The disloyal associate notices the good attributes of other ministers, but never speaks positively about his own pastor.**

A bad associate constantly notices the successes of outside ministers and praises them. But he is always complaining about the shortcomings of his own ministry. The fact is everyone has faults! If you have a critical attitude (third stage of disloyalty), you will notice 21 mistakes in everything your head does, a fact highlighted by the way the disloyal assistant notices and praises the good in other ministers.

**9. A subversive associate constantly listens to and learns from taped and videoed sermons from other ministers. But he never listens to his own head pastor's recorded teachings.**

Surely an associate must listen to the taped sermons of his own head pastor. Even though he is an associate and the next in rank, his senior is still his pastor. The feeding from the pulpit is a blessing even to assistant pastors. The fact that an associate feels he has nothing to learn from his senior pastor is a serious indicator. There is nothing wrong with assistants regularly learning from outside ministers. But there is something very wrong when associates never seem to want to learn from their own pastors.

### 10. A disaffected associate always feels that things should be done a different way.

As he watches his senior pastor, the disloyal assistant thinks to himself, "My pastor should have referenced more Scriptures when he was teaching." As he looks on during counseling sessions, he says to himself, "He's not handling this situation properly." He calmly observes his boss handling administrative issues, but he feels that there is a far better way of doing things. This is a mindset of discontentment and disloyalty. The disaffected associate is not happy and unconvinced about his leader's ministerial capabilities. I wouldn't want such an associate around me. I would never know what he is really thinking.

### 11. A disloyal associate is a habitual and persistent magnet for complaints.

Some members of the flock seem to find their way to such bad assistants with all sorts of complaints. Often they will say, "You are more approachable than the senior pastor." Watch out for these so-called "approachable" assistants.

### Department of Complaints

If I love my associates, I will not allow an environment where people feel free to say negative things to me about them. In the same way, if my associate is loyal, he will not allow anyone to readily speak evil of me to him. There will simply be no listening ear given to complaining and murmuring Christians. No one is perfect, and we all make many mistakes.

**If you are in effect the "complaint department" for a church or organization, there must be something wrong with you.** Why do people choose to come to you whenever they want to grumble or murmur about something?

### 12. They do not clap, smile, say "amen," shout or laugh when the head is preaching.

Disloyal assistants look like diplomatic "know-it-alls". They maintain straight and uninterested faces throughout a sermon. Certainly, a loyal and supportive associate would like to encourage his senior pastor to preach with great effect rather than making things more difficult. If your associates seem exuberant when others minister, but have unsmiling and rigid faces when you are ministering, there is something wrong.

### 13. A disloyal associate does not sing or lift up his hands during worship. Neither does he clap his hands during praise.

Disloyal associates hinder the flow and the work of the Spirit by their very rigid presence. Get rid of all such unhappy people who do not really want to be around. The church is better off without them.

### 14. A disloyal associate does not flow with the general mood of the congregation.

When everybody is laughing, he does not laugh. On a good day, he may afford a faint smile. When everybody is exclaiming in agreement, he may give a diplomatic nod of consent. When everybody's hands are raised, he will lift up only one hand. You see, he or she is simply not as impressed as the rest of the church.

### 15. A bad assistant is not happy at the wealth and blessings of his senior pastor.

This assistant feels the senior pastor has too much anyway. Disloyal associates feel they do the "donkey work" while the senior leader reaps all the rewards. In his heart, the assistant thinks, "Monkey dey work, baboon dey chop," as we say in Ghana. This assistant wants those same things himself.

### 16. A disloyal assistant openly disagrees with his head pastor.

Any associate who publicly displays disagreement with his pastor is sending a message to the whole church. Associates will frown, and you can see disapproval written all over their faces. What they are saying is, "I am opposed to the decisions that have been made. And I want everyone to know I was against it."

When an associate shows his disagreement publicly instead of waiting for a private forum to express his opinion, something is very wrong. He is undermining the authority of the pastor. Such a person is near the stage of full-blown rebellion because he no longer cares what people might think of his criticisms. Do you need me to tell you to get rid of this person?

**17. The disloyal associate considers the privileges and honors bestowed upon his senior pastor to be uncalled for and wasteful.**

Instead of seeing certain honors as appropriate and necessary privileges that accompany the position of senior pastor, they are constantly unhappy (whether openly or secretly) about any fame, respect and rights bestowed. They consider these as frivolous and a waste of resources. You will recall that the associate who thought in this way during the ministry of Jesus was the betrayer, Judas.

**18. They constantly have thoughts flashing through their mind about leaving the church.**

They may come to you and say they are confused as to whether or not they are in the will of God. When others are gladly receiving the sermon or teaching, they are contemplating whether or not to hand in their resignation. As they sit in pastoral board meetings, they hope in their hearts that they will not be around to implement decisions made during the meetings. Identify such assistants and be careful not to discuss with them your thoughts and plans for the future.

**19. Disaffected associates do not make any "extra" efforts!**

Take note when people make no "extra" efforts beyond their specified duties. A lazy and reluctant assistant is a dangerous liability. If a person is unhappy in what he is doing, he often does it listlessly and without enthusiasm. Watch the apathetic associates or workers around you. They may have already departed from you in their hearts.

**20. Traitorous associates listen to bad advice from "empty" and nonspiritual wives.**

Such a wife of an associate pastor is prone to stirring up discontent in her husband's mind. She passes comments and suggestions that make the assistant pastor feel dissatisfied with his rank and position. These "empty" wives think mainly of physical comfort, public impressions and their status in the church. They are often unaware of the spiritual implications of the advice they give.

A disloyal assistant is all ears to the carnal suggestions and pressure coming from his "empty" wife. There are many loyal leaders who disintegrate into disaffected and mutinous people because of the influences from their wives. The Bible teaches us that King Ahab was galvanized into doing much evil by his wife, Jezebel.

*...Ahab... whom Jezebel his wife stirred up.*   1 KINGS 21:25

# The Disloyal Assistant

*(For reasons of privacy you may want to make notes on a photocopy of this page.)*

## Chapter Eight- My Action Plan:

- **I AM an assistant.** Checkmark below the disloyal characteristics I am guilty of.
- **I HAVE an assistant.** Circle the check box below for the characteristics you have noticed in your assistant.
- Begin praying about how to change the disloyal thoughts and behaviors.

1. ☐ When things go wrong, unfaithful assistants are quick to say, "I knew all along that this would not work."
2. ☐ When you come up with a suggestion, new idea or vision they have no comment to make – either good or bad.
3. ☐ A disloyal assistant often thinks, "I would be a better leader than my superior if I just had the chance!"
4. ☐ A dissatisfied assistant is not happy about the differences between himself and his superior that make him look subordinate.
5. ☐ He is very concerned about his image rather than being concerned about raising the image of the one he assists.
6. ☐ A treacherous assistant will eagerly look for opportunities to walk in his leader's shoes.
7. ☐ The bad assistant sees all the faults and mistakes in the senior minister's life. He rarely sees the good things.
8. ☐ The disloyal associate notices the good attributes of other ministers, but never speaks positively about his own pastor.
9. ☐ A subversive associate constantly listens to and learns from taped and videoed sermons from other ministers. But he never listens to his own head pastor's recorded teachings.
10. ☐ A disaffected associate always feels that things should be done a different way.
11. ☐ A disloyal associate is a habitual and persistent magnet for complaints.

12. ☐ They do not clap, smile, say "amen," shout, or laugh when the head is preaching.

13. ☐ A disloyal associate does not sing or lift up his hands during worship. Neither does he clap his hands during praise.

14. ☐ A disloyal associate does not flow with the general mood of the congregation.

15. ☐ A bad assistant is not happy at the wealth and blessings of his senior pastor.

16. ☐ A disloyal assistant openly disagrees with his head pastor.

17. ☐ The disloyal associate considers the privileges and honors bestowed upon his senior pastor to be uncalled for and wasteful.

18. ☐ They constantly have thoughts flashing through their mind about leaving the church.

19. ☐ Disaffected associates do not make any "extra" efforts!

20. ☐ Traitorous associates listen to bad advice from "empty" and non-spiritual wives.

# CHAPTER 9

# Why Judas Betrayed Christ

I have always wondered why Judas betrayed his master, Jesus Christ. It is difficult to understand because we see Jesus as the King of Kings and the Lord of Lords. Why would anyone want to fight against God? Why would anyone want innocent blood on his hands?

Many people just see Judas Iscariot as a detestable person. Most refuse to name their children after Judas. But I believe many people were named Judas before the era of Christ.

I believe Judas was a trustworthy person when he started out. In fact, the Bible tells us that there was a point at which Satan entered into Judas. Thus there was a point in time when there was no devil in Judas.

### Judas: The Trusted Minister of Finance

If Judas weren't trustworthy, Jesus wouldn't have entrusted him with the money. **Most people appoint the most trustworthy person to be their treasurer.** I have appointed trustworthy people to be treasurers in my church or organizations, and I am sure you do the same. The Minister of Finance of any country must be very close and loyal to the Prime

Minister.

In this discussion, I want us to analyze what might have led Judas to betray Christ. Was this something that could have happened only to Judas? Or was it something that can happen to any of us?

### You Will Have a Judas

I remember once sitting with a senior church leader who said something that struck me! He said, "I don't care what leadership style you have. . . I don't care what type of leadership principles you are using. You are not greater than Jesus. If Jesus had a Judas, you will too!"

He went on, "No matter what you do, you will have to experience betrayal because your master experienced it."

This made me think deeply. I realized that what this senior minister said was true. Every church will have a Judas. Every church will experience the scourge of treacherous leaders.

*... it must needs be that offenses come...*   MATTHEW 18:7

**There will by all means be a Judas from among your trusted leadership.** The Bible describes him as a trusted friend who eats, drinks and fellowships with you. The Bible says that he is not an ordinary friend, but a familiar friend. That means someone who is very close.

*...mine own familiar friend, in whom I trusted, which did eat
of my bread, hath lifted up his heel against me.*   PSALM 41:9

Dear leader and pastor, you cannot escape this reality. I know it is difficult to believe that someone you may have known for years will fight against you one day.

Maybe you have not yet encountered this, but I assure you that as you become more experienced you will find out how true and accurate the Word of God is. I hardly know any seasoned minister who has not experienced betrayal in one form or another.

### Which of Us Will Be the Judas?

This truth has two implications. The implication for all senior leaders is simple. **Anticipate disloyalty and create a system that will not collapse in the event of betrayal.** Notice how Jesus' ministry continued effectively after Judas had fallen away. The implications for assistants, associates and followers is frightening, but also very real -- *one of us will be a Judas. Just make sure it's not you!*

> *...woe to that man by whom the offense cometh!*
> MATTHEW 18:7

The Apostle Paul knew it was inevitable that treacherous people would arise from among the congregation, so he said,

> *...after my departing shall grievous wolves enter...* ACTS 20:29

These grievous wolves are the anarchists and betrayers of the church. Other translations describe them as savage, monstrous, merciless, fierce and evil wolves. Paul said they would come!

I believe many people, though not called Judas, will behave like Judas when the opportunity presents itself. It's just a matter of time. As we begin this study, I want us to remember that Jesus prayed all night before he chose his 12 apostles.

You must also note that the disciples were very close to Jesus. They traveled together. They talked together, and they lived together.

How could someone so evil rise out of such a fraternity? The reasons I am going to share with you, although theoretical propositions, are very real. I think they apply especially to people who embark on full-time ministry or ministry as a career.

## 1. Judas was the odd man out.

All the disciples came from Galilee, *but Judas came from Kerioth.* **Judas was the exception to the Galilean team.** *He was the odd man out in a related Galilean family.* Whenever you are the exception or the odd person within a group, your oddness may cause you to see things in a different light. If you are the only black person among many whites, you may feel their jokes and comments are directed against your color.

### Who Is the Odd One Out?

If you are the only woman among men, you may tend to interpret their decisions as being targeted against women. If you are the only uneducated person among many educated people, the devil will come to you frequently and tell you that the people think you are stupid.

Watch out for people who are circumstantially peculiar. Judas probably began to see himself as different from the others. He gradually grew apart from the others as these thoughts raced through his mind. Many disloyal people are casualties of the "odd man out" experience.

## 2. Judas was disappointed at the type of training he was undergoing.

Judas initially felt that joining the ministry team would elevate his status and give him opportunities to minister. But to his surprise, he became an errand boy, a waiter, an usher and a scavenger.

> *Judas the Usher: And Jesus said, Make the men sit down...*
> JOHN 6:10

> *Judas the Waiter: ...the disciples [distributed food] to them that were set down...* JOHN 6:11

> *Judas the Errand Boy: ...then sent Jesus two disciples...*
> MATTHEW 21:1

> *Judas the Scavenger: ...Gather up the fragments that remain...*
> JOHN 6:12

### Judas Was Humiliated

Before thousands of people, Judas felt humiliated as he carried baskets of food from place to place. At some point Judas thought to himself, "This is not what I bargained for."

## 3. Judas was probably disappointed at the poor accommodations that the ministry office provided for him.

He thought that he would have better conditions of service. But in following Jesus he did not even have a good apartment or rented house to live in. In fact, he became a homeless street dweller.

> *...but the Son of man hath not where to lay his head.*
> LUKE 9:58

Judas thought to himself, "Jesus has not taken into consideration some important administrative details." Perhaps Judas hated staying with friends and crowding into people's homes. Imagine 12 grown men crowding into a small house.

> *And being In Bethany in the house of Simon the leper...*
> MARK 14:3

## 4. Judas was disappointed at the poor transportation provided by the ministry office.

Perhaps Judas thought that by going into full-time ministry, he would have the luxury of owning his own donkey or mule (car). This was not to be. The only person to ride on a donkey was Jesus himself, and even that was at the end of his ministry.

> *...thy King [Jesus] cometh... sitting upon an ass [donkey]...*
> MATTHEW 21:5

What a disappointment for the aspiring young man! A number of people defect from their ministry jobs when they discover that good cars are not as readily available as they had imagined. What is even more difficult for them is when only the Chief Executive (the Lord Jesus, in the case of Judas) seems to enjoy certain benefits.

## 5. Perhaps Judas was not happy with the type of food he had to eat when he became a full-time minister.

Judas was probably looking forward to some good restaurants and expensive, high quality food. Judas likely thought that he had enjoyed better times when he was not working for Christ.

**No Chinese Restaurants?**

He Judas had hoped for some good Chinese dinners with international guests. But the worst came when he was asked to eat other people's leftovers.

> *...and filled twelve baskets with the fragments [leftovers]...*
> *which remained over and above unto them that had eaten.*
> JOHN 6:13

**6. Perhaps Judas began to see Jesus as a wicked miser who would never be generous to his employees.**

This point was emphasized when Jesus asked his disciples to collect the leftover crumbs. As Judas carried his basket of crumbs, he must have thought to himself, "This is the end! I cannot take this stingy treatment any longer."

> *...Gather up the fragments that remain...*   JOHN 6:12

**7. Perhaps Judas did not like the special way Jesus was being treated.**

He thought that the expense being lavished on Christ was unnecessary. "Who is this Christ anyway?" he thought. Why spend so much money on one man? There are 13 of us on the team now. Why single out one person and expend so much on him? After all, we started this ministry together a few years ago. He began to believe there was an imbalance in the distribution of church finances.

> *...To what purpose is this waste?*   MATTHEW 26:8

**8. Perhaps Judas felt that the emphasis and direction of the ministry had changed.**

Maybe he felt that more money should be given to the poor. As treasurer, Judas knew how money was being spent in the ministry. He now viewed Jesus' financial and administrative policies to be defective.

> *Why was not this... given to the poor?*   JOHN 12:5

## 9. Maybe Judas had accused Jesus of misusing the church's finances.

I want to tell you a secret -- a revelation that you must always remember. The person who tenaciously accuses others of horrible crimes, is often guilty of the same. A person who has never been involved in some sin usually doesn't accuse others in an adamant fashion. This is because those evil crimes do not even come to his mind as options that he could take.

### He Accused His Wife Continually

I remember a man who continually accused his wife of adultery. He would say to her, "I know you. You are going out with another man." But she was doing nothing of the sort. Ironically, this man was having multiple affairs with different women.

It was Judas who accused Jesus of wasting and misusing the church's money. And it was Judas himself who was the thief.

> *...he [Judas] was a thief...* JOHN 12:6

## 10. Perhaps Judas wanted to get rich quickly.

Maybe Judas thought his income was too low for the work he did. Even though Jesus promised that those who followed him would have car loans and housing benefits, he couldn't imagine how or when such a promise would materialize.

> *...he shall receive an hundredfold now in this time, houses...*
> MARK 10:30

So he began to think of other means to get money quickly. He began by stealing money from the offering.

> *...he [Judas] was a thief...* JOHN 12:6

After a while this was not enough. He felt a big one-time deal would earn him a lot of money. Considering the hatred the Jews had for Christ, he realized that if he could sell off Christ, he could make it in a big way.

> *And Judas... went unto the chief priests, to betray him unto*

*them... they were glad, and promised to give him money...*
MARK 14:10, 11

### 11. Perhaps Judas had become too familiar with Christ.

There is a saying, "familiarity breeds contempt." It's not in the Bible but it is true. Judas had now been with Jesus for three years. He had seen Jesus happy.

*...Jesus rejoiced...* LUKE 10:21

He had seen Jesus crying.

*Jesus wept.* JOHN 11:35

Judas knew Christ not only in his moments of great power, miracles and anointing, he also knew him when he was vulnerable, like any other man. Judas would not have attempted to murder Christ if he did not view him as an ordinary human being.

*...mine own familiar friend... hath lifted up his heel against me.* PSALM 41:9

Familiarity had crept in as Judas engaged in so many day-to-day activities with his master. He had been with Jesus as he ate. He had been with Jesus when he went to the restroom. The close fellowship that Judas had with Jesus led him to believe that he could easily be betrayed or even killed. Judas did not see Jesus as God, but as man. Nobody in his or her right mind would attempt to betray God. But many would attempt to betray another man.

As soon as you begin to see your "man of God" -- your pastor or spiritual mentor -- as a mere man, you will no longer receive from him the same. Evil thoughts of betrayal can now enter your mind. Ministers must therefore not allow themselves to become too familiar.

*...mine own familiar friend...* PSALM 41:9

The congregation as a whole must also not want to become too familiar with their ministers. This reduces the temptations familiarity brings.

**12. Perhaps Judas realized that Jesus had discovered he was a thief.**

It was a known fact (even before Christ was crucified) that Judas was a thief.

> *...but because he [Judas] was a thief...* JOHN 12:6

Was giving up the Lord an opportunity for Judas to get away clean? Some government officials, when they realize that their corruption has been uncovered, decide to burn down their entire office in an attempt to destroy all relevant documents and evidence. Judas probably realized that he had been discovered and feared that he would be exposed further. He decided that he would attack Jesus before anything happened to him.

**Many rebels are guilty of other crimes in addition to rebellion.** They often time use their rebellion to cover up other offenses. Judas timed his betrayal to exterminate Christ before he could publicly disgrace him. Some ministers, fearing public discipline for their wrongdoing, fight against authority. They pretend to have justifiable reasons for doing so. But behind the façade are many shameful crimes.

### He Attacked Me First

I remember the bitter attacks of one minister against my life and ministry. As I mused over all the lies and unbelievable stories this gentleman spread about me, I realized it was just an attempt to cover his own shame. As we say in Ghana, "Do them before they do you."

**13. Perhaps Judas thought that if Jesus was to really die he would lose his job. He had to secure himself.**

Judas decided the future was not so bright. With the impending departure of Christ, he conceived a plan that would give him enough money to set up a private business.

> *And Judas... went unto the chief priests, to betray him unto them... they were glad, and promised to give him money...*
> MARK 14:10, 11

Perhaps Judas thought that if he were to betray Christ and earn some money, it would stabilize his family financially for the next few years.

### 14. Perhaps Judas knew too much about too many things.

He knew about the offerings.

> *...he [Judas]... had the bag [account book], and bare what was put therein.* JOHN 12:6

Judas knew how much money came into the ministry. He knew Jesus' timetable. He knew where Jesus lived and when he traveled. Sometimes what people know does not help them because they see things from the wrong perspective. Be careful about those who count the church's money. Those who count often do not pay the church bills. They just know the income of the church, but not the expenses.

> *...neither do I exercise myself in great matters, or in things too high for me.* PSALM 131:1

Thus, they may have a false idea about the kind of wealth the church has. This can foster disloyalty and treachery.

### 15. Perhaps he [Judas] thought that the power and anointing on Jesus Christ was waning because Jesus kept talking about his death.

Usually only depressed people keep talking about death. Jesus Christ calmly predicted his death several times.

> *And he began to teach them, that the Son of man must suffer... and be killed...* MARK 8:31

Each time Jesus talked about the end of his ministry, Judas must have thought, "The fight has gone out of this man. He is not as powerful as he was three years ago."

"When I first knew this man, he would powerfully confront the Pharisees and Sadducees. He would preach with such zeal. No one could stand before the anointed preaching of Christ," he remembered. "Things have changed. The anointing has lifted."

Many natural people observe a man of God with a very critical eye.

They notice variations in his mood and presentation of the Word. Over a long period, such critical observers may conclude that the man of God is in a "low" season.

### Don't Make a Mistake

There may be a genuine change in a minister's outlook because God may have moved him on to another phase of his ministry. But make no mistake about this: it does not mean that God is not with him.

When Jesus cried, "O God why hast thou forsaken me," many thought he was an ordinary man who had come to an unfortunate demise. Little did they know that this was just a stage in the ministry of the Lord Jesus Christ. **Unfortunately, Judas totally misinterpreted the phase and change in Jesus' ministry.**

# Why Judas Betrayed Christ

*(For reasons of privacy you may want to make notes on a photocopy of this page.)*

## Chapter Nine- My Action Plan:

1. What one or two thoughts about Judas caught my attention as I read?

2. Do I know a "Judas?" What are the clues?

3. If the truth were known, am I a "Judas?"

## CHAPTER 10

# How to Avoid Disloyalty

How can we escape from the dangers of disloyal betrayal? I believe one of the ways is to learn how honorably to leave a church or organization without rebelling. I call this godly resignation.

### Godly Resignation

Leaving a church or ministry (resigning, in other words) happens whether we like it or not. Most of the time people never intend to leave. However, there are reasons why resignation occurs.

### Resignation Is Rarely Peaceful

Resignation is rarely done in a cordial atmosphere. Resignation in the church setting usually comes as the result of misunderstandings, conflicts, accusations and unhealed wounds. I am sorry to say, I have rarely seen a truly peaceful departure.

I believe there are three reasons why departure (or resignation) may be biblically necessary:

    i. When it comes as an explicit instruction from the Lord.

ii. When there is a major doctrinal deviation in the ministry.

iii. When there is a significant and chronic moral deviation.

Why is it important to leave a ministry that is suffering from major doctrinal or moral decay? That wrong spirit is likely to eventually affect you.

If you have to resign, there are certain standards of behavior expected of you before, during and after your resignation. How you go about your departure will show everyone whether you are a faithful worker or just another anarchist.

a) Give ample notice of your intentions to leave the ministry or church. *Ample notice means at least one year.*

b) *Resignation must never be a surprise move.* If it comes as a surprise, then it is an evil, calculated misdeed.

c) If you must resign, resign alone. *Do not try to influence others to leave with you.*

d) Do not try to win the hearts of people long before you leave such as by making special friends all around and developing close relationships with vital church members.

In the end you will leave behind a confused group of members who have to choose between their relationship with you and their commitment to the church. This is another reason why you need to declare your intentions to resign long beforehand.

e) Be grateful to the church from where you are departing, and *do not spread bad stories about them after you leave.*

> *Whoso rewardeth evil for good, evil shall not depart from his house.* PROVERBS 17:13

f) Do not "muddy" the waters you have drunk from by leaving behind a group of confused people.

By saying evil things about the church you have just left, you "muddy" the waters and prevent others from being trained and blessed by the same ministry, which had blessed you.

> *Seemeth it a small thing unto you to have eaten up the good pasture, but ye must tread down with your feet the residue of your pastures? And to have drunk of the deep waters, but ye*

*must foul the residue with your feet?* EZEKIEL 34:18

This will invite a curse into your life. It cannot possibly be that the church you were trained in has become such an evil place. **The reason why most ministers disappear into oblivion after departure from a major ministry is because they bring upon themselves a curse by the manner in which they leave.**

g) If you intend to set up a church, you must declare your intentions to the senior minister. *You must, however, discourage others from following you.*

h) Do not set up a church anywhere within a 10-mile radius *from where you used to be.*

i) It is improper, cheap and unethical to establish a church virtually next door to your mother church.

j) *It also smacks of the logic of the jungle* to use the same or very similar names that are unique to the church or ministry you are leaving.

*The new name should in no way be a reminder of your recent defection.* For instance, if the church you resigned from is called *Angels Harvest and Healing Center International,* do not call your new church *Angels Salvation and Healing Center International.*

k) After departure you must speak well about where you came from. This will give you some credibility.

## The Jacob Style

Notice that Jacob resigned from Laban's ministry in the wrong way. He left unexpectedly. His absence was undetected for three days. Jacob almost received a curse for this.

> *And Jacob stole away unawares to Laban the Syrian, in that he told him not that he fled. So he fled with all that he had; and he rose up, and passed over the river, and set his face toward the mount Gilead. And it was told Laban on the third day that Jacob was fled.* GENESIS 31:20-22

But for God's intervention, Laban could have spoken a curse on Jacob (v. 29).

### The Moses Style

Observe that Moses on the other hand, left his father-in-law, Jethro's ministry in the right way. He had been with him for 40 years. Notice also that when it mattered, many years later, he could receive help from, and relate to Jethro.

> And Moses went and returned to Jethro his father in law, and said unto him, Let me go, I pray thee, and return unto my brethren which are in Egypt, and see whether they be yet alive. And Jethro said to Moses, Go in peace.    EXODUS 4:18

> And Moses went out to meet his father in law... and they asked each other of their welfare; and they came into the tent... And it came to pass on the morrow, that Moses sat to judge the people: and the people stood by Moses from the morning unto the evening.  Hearken now unto my [Jethro] voice, I will give thee counsel, and God shall be with thee...   EXODUS 18:7, 13, 19

Moses' method of departure from his ministry in the desert is more ethical. It was followed by blessings many years later. Let us learn from these lessons. It is my prayer that you would read over these truths repeatedly. In doing so, I believe that the Lord will give you an even greater understanding of how to behave in the Kingdom.

> ...that thou mayest know HOW THOU OUGHTEST TO BEHAVE THYSELF in the house of God...   1 TIMOTHY 3:15

### Can Rebels Repent?

Is there any hope for the person who gets involved with betrayal?

I believe not every traitor is deeply rebellious. Some are innocent and some are not. Let me point out to you that it was not only Judas who deserted Christ in his last hours. Every single disciple, except John the beloved, disowned Christ when it mattered most. There were a few people standing at the cross in the heat of the crisis: John the beloved, Mary the mother of Jesus, and Mary Magdalene. The other disciples were nowhere to be found.

> *Now there stood by the cross of Jesus his mother, and his mother's*
> *sister, Mary the wife of Cleophas, and Mary Magdalene. When*
> *Jesus therefore saw his mother, and the disciple standing by,*
> *whom he loved, he saith unto his mother...* JOHN 19:25, 26

Peter cursed and denied ever having had anything to do with Christ. In spite of this, the fate of Peter was very different from the fate of Judas. I believe Peter's desertion was not of the heart, but it was an emotional and irrational action that might be expected of most people in his circumstance.

And what about Judas? Didn't he repent? The Bible says that he went back to the High Priest saying that he had betrayed innocent blood.

> *And he cast down the pieces of silver... and went and hanged*
> *himself.* MATTHEW 27:5

He did admit that he had done something wrong. Is this not repentance? No, that was not repentance. I have often wondered why Judas is considered not to have genuinely repented. The answer is simple. **Judas admitted that he was wrong, but he did not retrace his steps.**

To repent means to turn around, and to change. Judas never changed. He did not turn around or retrace his steps. He just admitted that he was wrong, jumped out of the boat and hung himself! He did not want to see anybody or face anyone. He just excused himself.

He could not bear to look at the faces of the other disciples and admit to them that he was wrong. I have seen pastors admit one or two mistakes that they have made. But that did not amount to repentance. Remember what I said earlier: admission of sins is not the same as repenting. Many people who come up with apologies have a "what did they say I should say" attitude.

### She asked, "What Did They Say I Should Say?"

There was a disagreement between a husband and a wife. The problem got so bad that the families had to intervene. After much discussion, it was discovered that the wife was at fault. The council of elders asked the lady to apologize to the family and especially to her husband.

She grudgingly agreed and went from elder to elder saying to them, "I'm sorry for what I did." When she got to her husband, with a bored look on her face, she turned around to ask the others, "What did they say I should say to him?"

Dear reader, in asking this question she confirmed that she indeed had not repented. She was only being forced to admit her mistakes. Never forget that true repentance is different from admitting one's sins.

I was discussing with a pastor friend what to do if a rebellious separatist came back claiming he had repented from his sins. We agreed that the following seven points would help to differentiate between a forced admission of wrongdoing and true godly repentance.

1. First of all, admit to yourself and to God that you have been a rebel.
2. Ask God for his mercy and forgiveness.
3. Confess your rebellion to those against whom you rebelled.
4. Tell your rebel group that you have realized that you were a rebel. Explain to them your decision to repent.
5. Go to the church from which you rebelled and confess your sins publicly.
6. Confess to any other parties that were involved during the time of your rebellion.
7. Those from whom you rebelled will forgive you for your rebellion and release you to God's blessing.

# How to Avoid Disloyalty

*(For reasons of privacy you may want to make notes on a photocopy of this page.)*

## Chapter Ten- My Action Plan:

- What friend or associate of mine in ministry should I share these insights with about how to resign in a godly way?

- I am (or am considering) resigning my present position. Checkmark which of the behaviors below, during and after my resignation, I must be careful to observe (or those I might ignore).
    1. ☐ Give ample notice of your intentions to leave the ministry or church. Ample notice means at least one year.
    2. ☐ Resignation must never be a surprise move.
    3. ☐ Resign alone. Do not try to influence others to leave with you.
    4. ☐ Do not try to win the hearts of people long before you leave.
    5. ☐ Be grateful to the church you are departing from. Do not spread bad stories about them after you leave.
    6. ☐ Do not "muddy" the waters you have drunk from by leaving behind a group of confused people.

# CHAPTER 11

# The North Wind

*The north wind driveth away rain: so doth an angry counte-*
*nance a backbiting tongue.* PROVERBS 25:23

I n nature, a north wind drives away clouds, thereby preventing unnecessary problems from storms. In the church and our organizations,
we need to drive away certain potential storms from our midst. Many
people do not realize that a little leaven leavens the whole lump.

*...Know ye not that a little leaven leaveneth the whole lump?*
1 CORINTHIANS 5:6

It takes only a little venom to kill a six-foot tall, 80-kilogram man. In
other words, the whole body can be polluted or destroyed by one drop of
poison. Many businessmen do not understand that by retaining certain
employees, they are destroying their firms.

When someone hates you, there is very little you can do about it. The
best thing to do is to ask the person to be separate from you. It is time to
create an airtight culture in your organization -- an organization that is
unfriendly to scoffers and disloyal people!

If you live in a culture where people do not speak their minds, this is very important. You may have people smiling at you all the time and passing pleasant remarks. But this means nothing if in reality, they don't believe in you.

In South Africa, I frequently noticed a sign at the front of many public buildings. It said, "Right of Admission Reserved." It meant that they had the right to exclude anyone whose presence was not desirable. I believe the church has a right to exclude people whose presence is not desirable. God is love, and the environment that must prevail in the church is love! **Anything or anyone who consistently destroys the atmosphere of love within a church should be driven away in the same way that a north wind drives away unnecessary storms.**

*These are spots in your feasts of charity...* JUDE 12

Who are these "spots in your feasts of charity?" What are these intrusions that disturb the environment of Christian love, peace and harmony? Read verse 10 of the Book of Jude and you will see for yourself.

> *But these SPEAK EVIL OF THOSE THINGS WHICH*
> *THEY KNOW NOT: but what they know naturally, as brute*
> *beasts, in those things they corrupt themselves. Woe unto them!*
> *For they have gone in the way of Cain, and ran greedily after*
> *the error of Balaam for the reward, and perished in the gainsay-*
> *ing of Core. THESE ARE SPOTS in your feasts of charity...*
> *CARRIED ABOUT OF WINDS...* JUDE 10-12

If these spots in our feasts of love can be carried by winds, it shows how insubstantial they are. It is time for a north wind to blow these things away.

You could actually call a north wind **the wind of exclusion.** Here are examples of people who may have to be blown away by the north wind of exclusion.

### The Wind of Exclusion
**1. A backbiting tongue must be flushed out of the church.**

A backbiting person bites your back. In other words, he or she does not have the boldness to speak to your face. He has to wait for your back to be turned. Such people are dangerous. They are potential Absaloms. When discovered, they should repent or be flushed out.

## 2. A slanderer must be driven away from the church.

Slander comes from the Hebrew word "Lashan". It means to use the tongue to defame, abuse, scandalize, belittle or blacken the character of another. King David was slandered by many people. Do you need people to blacken your character? Certainly not!

> *I am forgotten as a dead man out of mind: I am like a broken vessel. For I have heard the slander of many: fear was on every side: while they took counsel together against me, they devised to take away my life.*  PSALM 31:12, 13

Why was David like a broken vessel because of slander? Many ministers are like broken vessels, which can no longer hold the anointing. If slander has such a terrible effect on God's chosen vessels, then it must not be entertained at all!

## 3. A double-tongued person must be driven away from the church.

> *Likewise must the deacons be grave, not double-tongued...*
> 1 TIMOTHY 3:8

## 4. A murmurer must be driven away from the church.

> *Do all things without murmurings and disputings...*
> PHILIPPIANS 2:14

People who speak in undertones and bring a spirit of unwillingness are dangerous people. It is very difficult to lead unwilling and discouraged people.

## 5. Evil "critics" must be driven away from the church.

**6. Talebearers must be driven from the church.**

Talebearers are people who invent stories or recreate events to make them look unwholesome. Such people separate friends and pollute the environment with an unhealthy poison. They must be driven away from the church.

> *Where no wood is, there the fire goeth out: so where there is no talebearer, the strife ceaseth. As coals are to burning coals, and wood to fire; so is a contentious man to kindle strife. The words of a talebearer are as wounds, and they go down into the innermost parts of the belly.* PROVERBS 26:20-22

Notice that the Bible says that where there is no talebearer there is no strife. In other words, if you want to get rid of strife, get rid of the talebearers.

**7. Accusers must be driven away from the church.**

The devil's nature is to accuse. Anyone who rises up with a spirit of accusation is actually representing the devil. One of the most appropriate names for the devil is "accuser of the brethren." In the church, there are always people who allow themselves to be used as accusers. Such people create stories that look very true but are not, and they end up sowing seeds of confusion in the church. Accusers must be driven out!

**8. Liars must be driven away from the church.**

I remember one young man who made it his duty to tell lies about me. This gentleman would not leave the church. He wanted to be with us and still malign us constantly. One day, one of the pastors in the church just asked him to leave. It seems he did not know how to leave the church. People do not realize that if you are not happy with what pertains in the church, you should simply move away without destroying the church of Christ.

**9. People who cause divisions must be driven away from the church.**

*Now I beseech you, brethren, mark them which cause divisions and offenses contrary to the doctrine which ye have learned; and avoid them.* ROMANS 16:17

It is sometimes important to take a good spiritual history. You will learn what people have done in every church they have been in. Dear pastors, don't be overly excited when you receive a member from another church. Find out why he moved. Problems that person was associated with in the old place will surely come up again!

## 10. People who cause quarrels.

*...them which cause divisions and offenses...* ROMANS 16:17

Some people are always causing offenses and quarrels. These are contentious individuals. They delight in magnifying frivolous or vexing issues until these become a pivot for divisions. It is important to mark these people and avoid them.

# The North Wind

*(For reasons of privacy you may want to make notes on a photocopy of this page.)*

## Chapter Eleven- My Action Plan:

- Is the culture of my church or organization one where people are not free to speak their mind? List three evidences:

  1.

  2.

  3.

- Is your church or organizational culture appropriately unfriendly to scoffers and disloyal people?

- Ask God for wisdom to identify persons in your church or organization that must be "blown away by the north wind of exclusion." Pray for clarity of insight and God's leading in any action you contemplate.

  Bishop Heward-Mills listed these qualities:
  1. A person with a backbiting tongue
  2. A slanderer
  3. A double-tongued person
  4. A murmurer
  5. An evil "critic"
  6. A talebearer
  7. An accuser
  8. A liar
  9. A person who causes divisions
  10. A person who causes quarrels

# CHAPTER 12

# The Good Fruit of Loyalty

*...Well done, thou good and faithful servant: thou hast been faithful over a few things. I will make thee ruler over many things: enter thou into the joy of thy Lord.* MATTHEW 25:21

This Scripture outlines two important blessings that follow loyal, faithful people. They receive an increase (many things) from the Lord. As you pray for growth in your church and ministry, remember that loyalty is the master key to expansion. Loyalty allows and helps you to persist in the same thing until it bears fruit.

I suggest that you engage in a little research. You will discover that large growing churches differ in style, strategy and emphasis. Some are soul-winning churches; others have an emphasis on miracles and the Holy Spirit. Some mega-churches are oriented toward social services and political issues. Still other large churches have an emphasis on prosperity and dominion! All of these churches differ greatly in many areas. However, a closer look will reveal that there are some common denominators between every large church.

Almost all large churches are led by pastors who have remained faithful to the same church for a considerable time. When pastors move every few years, they do not experience consistent growth. If you are a minister who desires expansion and growth, you must be prepared to stay in one place for a long time. Ask God for the privilege of investing your entire life in one location.

I am in the ministry for the rest of my life. My commitment to the people around me is a lifetime commitment and vice versa. I am loyal to them and I pray that they will be loyal to me. The blessing of largeness is reserved for faithful and loyal people.

The second blessing of faithfulness is entering the joy of the Lord. This means experiencing the favor of God. When the favor of God is upon you, your enemies will not flourish.

> *By this I know that thou favourest me, because mine enemy doth not triumph over me.* PSALM 41:11

Be a loyal person so that you can have great growth in your business or ministry. Be a loyal person so that you can have God's favor over all that you set your hand to do.

May you one day hear those coveted words, "Well done, good and faithful (loyal) servant." May you experience the good fruits and benefits that belong to every faithful Christian!

# Other Books in the Loyalty and Disloyalty Series
## By Dag Heward-Mills

*Those Who Leave You*
*Those Who Pretend*
*Those Who Accuse You*
*Those Who Forget*

# Bishop Dag Heward-Mills:
## Shining Radiant Arcs of Light World-wide

He has been called a "faithful servant," an "inspiration to Christianity" and a "ray of hope and healing" to the lost and hurting around the world. Many have compared his passion for sharing the Gospel to the brilliant beam of a lighthouse, "his eyes burning with a vision" that illumines the Way for millions of seekers across the globe.

Indeed, over the past 20 years, evangelist, pastor and author Dag Heward-Mills has impacted millions through a multi-faceted world-wide ministry—one that shines with many amazing, bold arcs of light. An array of soul-winning projects, all of which he leads, directs or has written, are woven together to create a powerful force for Christ. And today they continue to gain brilliance and momentum.

These bright, evangelistic embers can be traced back to a time decades ago. Born in the UK to a Ghanaian lawyer and Swiss mother and growing up in the West African coastal country of Ghana, Dag gave his life to the Lord as a teenager. Soon after, while completing a seven-year training program at the University of Ghana Medical School, he felt God anointing him to teach and, testifying to God's fervent call on his life, began holding meetings in a campus classroom. As attendance swelled, meetings were moved to larger and larger rooms—and thus the first Lighthouse Chapel was born. Meanwhile, Dag earned his medical degree in 1989 and was ordained into the ministry in London the following year. Six years later, in 1996, the International Ministerial Council of Great Britain consecrated him as bishop.

Through all these occurrences, one of many sweeps of light began to intensely shine. As more churches were planted under Dag's leadership as presiding bishop, Lighthouse Chapel International (LCI) grew into a world-wide denomination with almost 1300 churches spreading across every continent in 60 countries, including 63 churches in the United States. Back in Accra, Ghana (LCI's home base), Bishop Heward-Mills commissioned in 2006 the construction of one of the largest church complexes in Africa—called the Qodesh (the Hebrew word for consecrated, dedicated or Holy Hill)—where attendance today often overflows its capacity.

Yet another gleaming glint of light appeared in 2004 when Dag held an evangelistic event, sparking the much-acclaimed Healing Jesus Crusades across Africa and other third-world countries. Today, this ministry seems to glow with God's blessing. Picture massive crowds gathering, listening and responding to the truth of God's Word, with thousands committing their lives to Christ and others receiving healing in His name. While the first crusade drew just over 600 attendees, each gathering now attracts up to five hundred thousand at each event.

To follow up each crusade, faith-building books and pamphlets written by Bishop Heward-Mills are freely "seeded" to help disciple and lead throngs of new believers to a closer walk with Christ. In fact, the Bishop is now known as a prolific author, with more than 73 titles to date, including 30 international bestsellers and many new releases anticipated in the coming months (including the much-acclaimed 5-book series *Loyalty and Disloyalty*). These books, including bestseller *The Art of the Follower* and many others, help pastors build stronger churches and motivate readers to effectively bolster their ministries, families and marriages.

Still other lights sparkle in multiple arenas—inspiring the next generation to ministry, healing the sick and rescuing orphans from lives of pain and abuse. In 1995, the Bishop established the Lighthouse Christian Mission Schools and, in 1997, added the Anagkazo Bible and Ministry Training Center. In 2006, he established three more rays of hope: the Lighthouse Mission Hospital, the Healing Jesus Medical Missions and the Lighthouse Christian Orphanage. Partnering with other ministries, Dag and his dedicated team are helping communities around the globe.

The list continues. He has held multiple conferences to equip church leaders, serves on the board of Church Growth International and produces radio and TV programs, DVD's and CD's, all to share the Gospel world-wide. He has also teamed up with his wife, Adelaide, to speak to crowds across Africa on the importance of a strong, faith-filled marriage and its vital role in the life of a Christian.

The blessed parents of four wonderful children—David, Joshua, Daniella and Paula—Dag and Adelaide reside in Accra, Ghana, where their passion for outreach continues to radiantly shine. Indeed, the Bishop and his ministry team have set robust goals, which include "to build 25,000 churches in 150 countries," "to continue to fight fiercely and relentlessly in all battles for the advancement of the churches and the Gospel" and "to produce passionate Christians who work for God."

Perhaps a final goal, in its simplicity, proves the most telling: "to go to Heaven and hear Jesus say, 'Well done, good and faithful servant.'" Looking back, Bishop Dag Heward-Mills may indeed see many arcs of light all intertwined—a unified beam cutting through the darkness as millions are enlightened with the hope of the Gospel. Until then, the "faithful servant" stands in the lighthouse, shining the Way.

www.daghewardmills.org